31 Countdown To Halloween Coloring Book

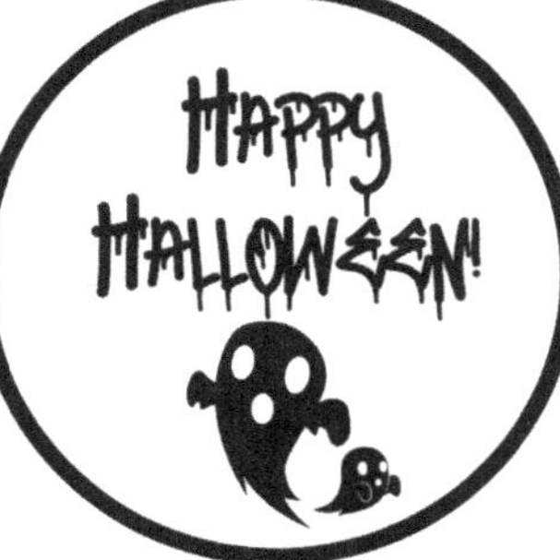

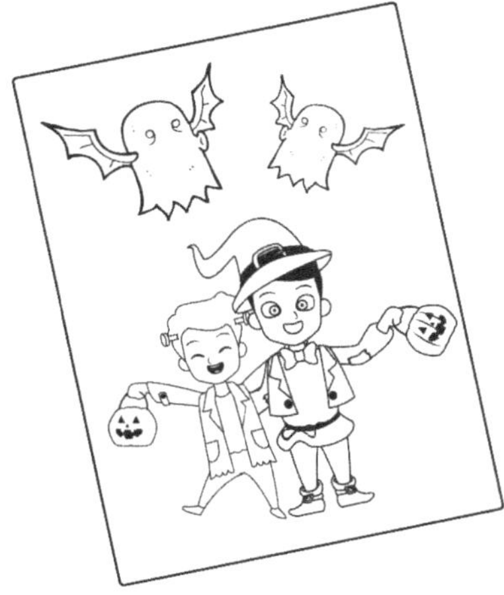

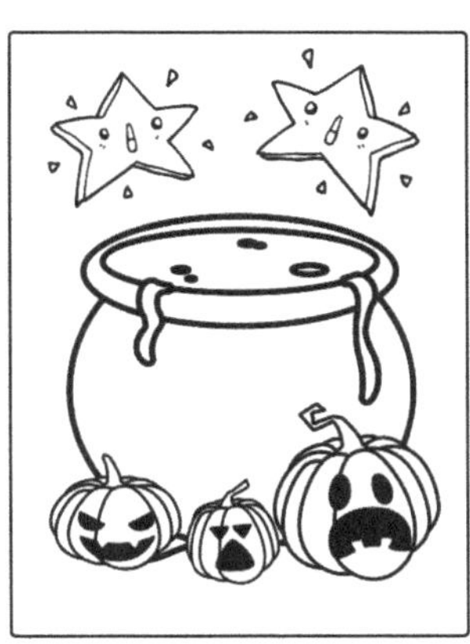

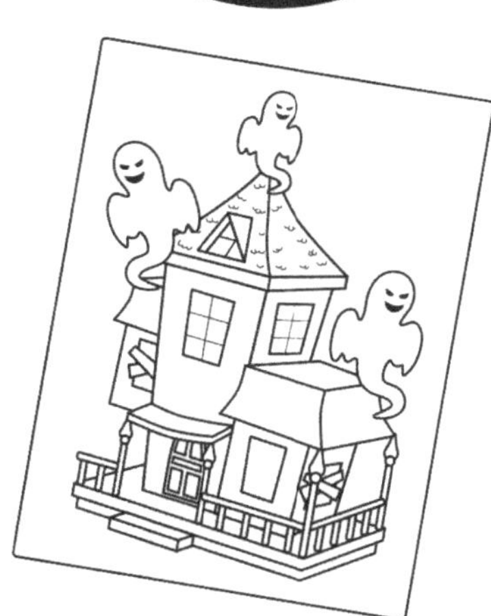

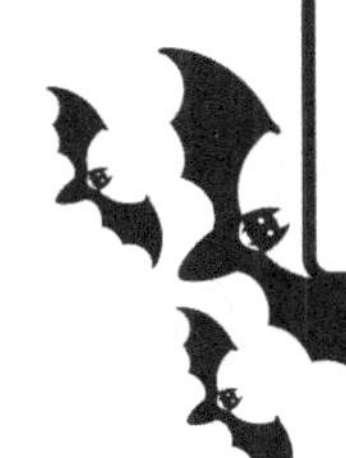

This Book Belonges To:

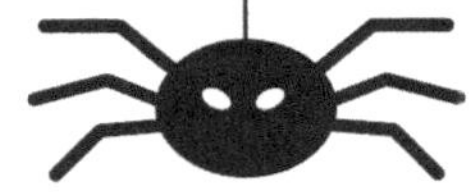

....

CLAREN SMILE

THANK YOU FOR PURCHASING MY BOOK

IF YOU ENJOY USING THIS BOOK, I WOULD APPRECIATE OF YOUR
REVIEW ON AMAZON.
JUST HEAD ON OVER THE BOOK'S AMAZON PAGE AND CLICK
"WRITE A CUSTOMER REVIEW"

I WALUE MY CUSTOMERS AND ALWAYS WELCOME SUGGESTIONS AND
FEEDBACK.

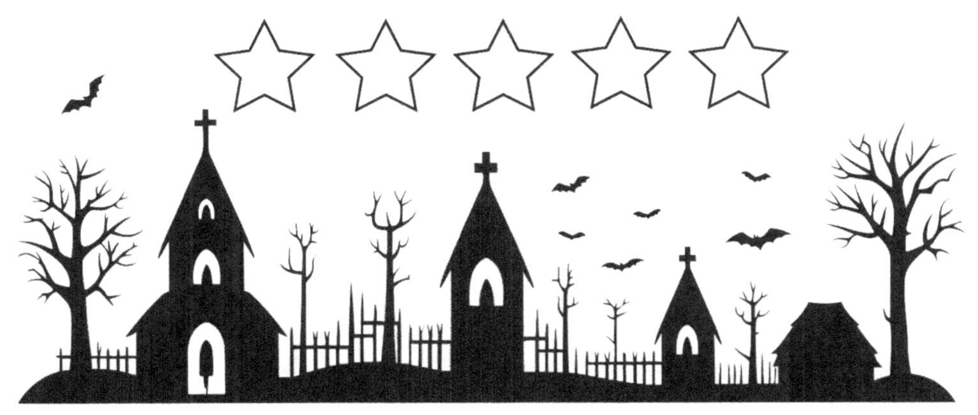

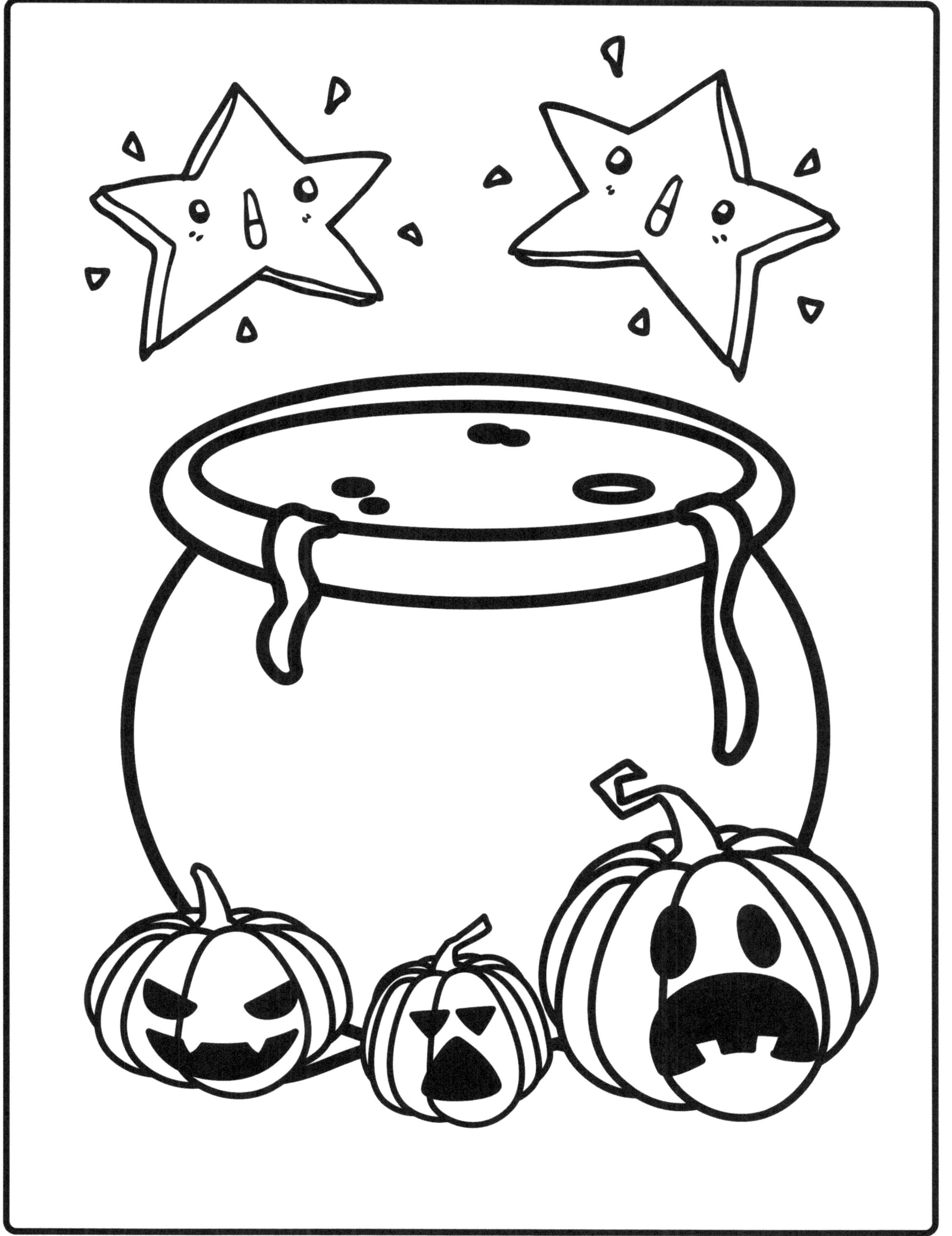

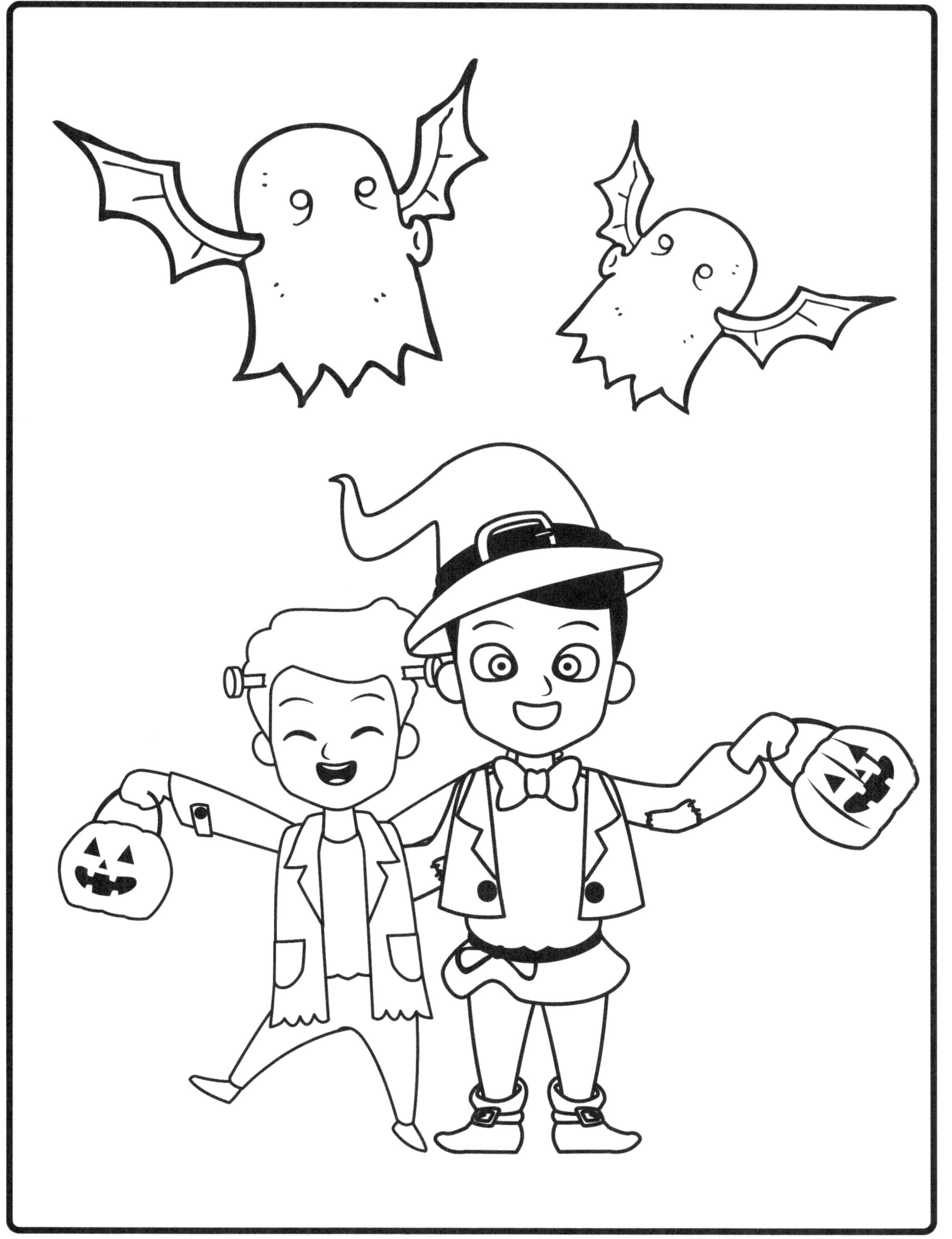

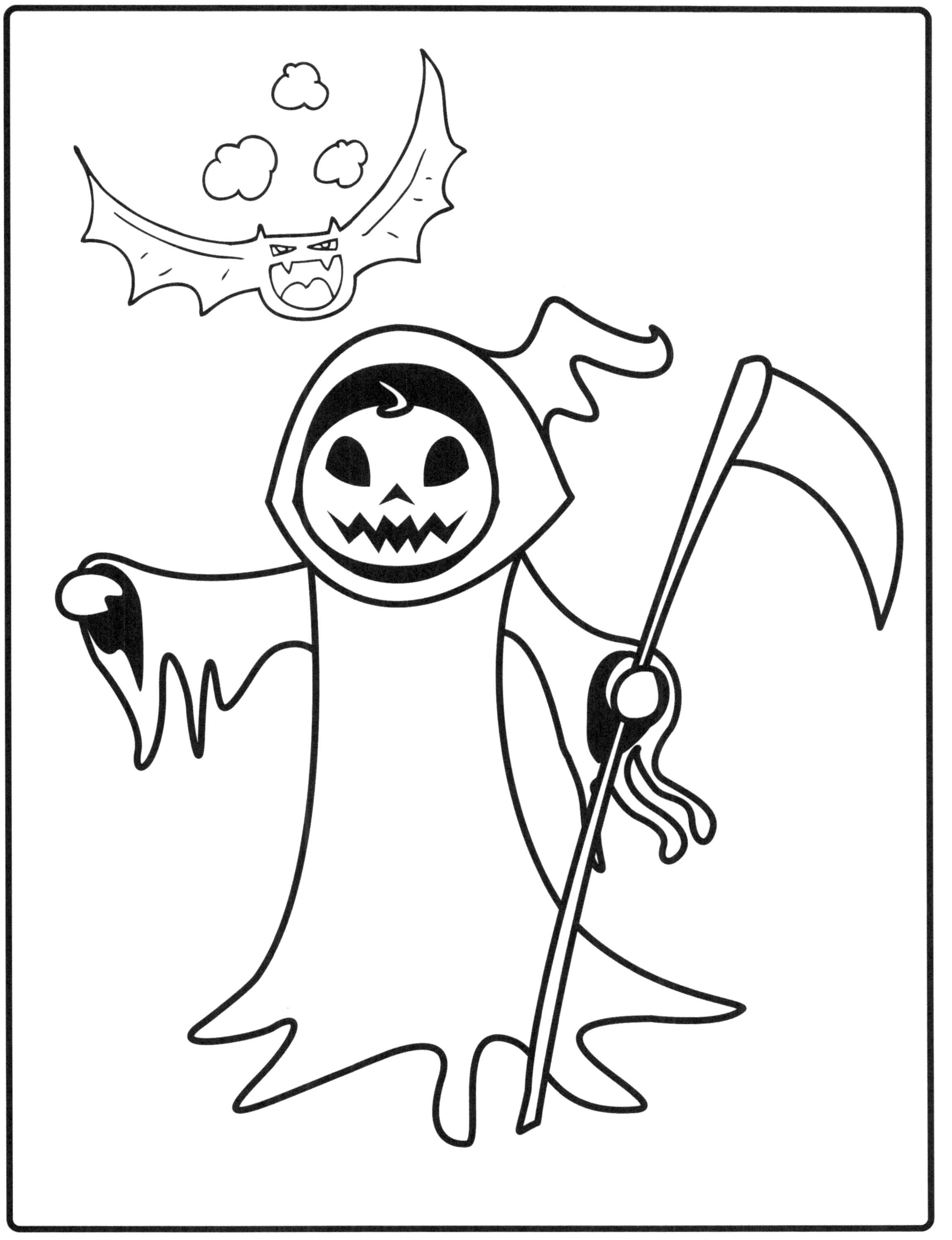

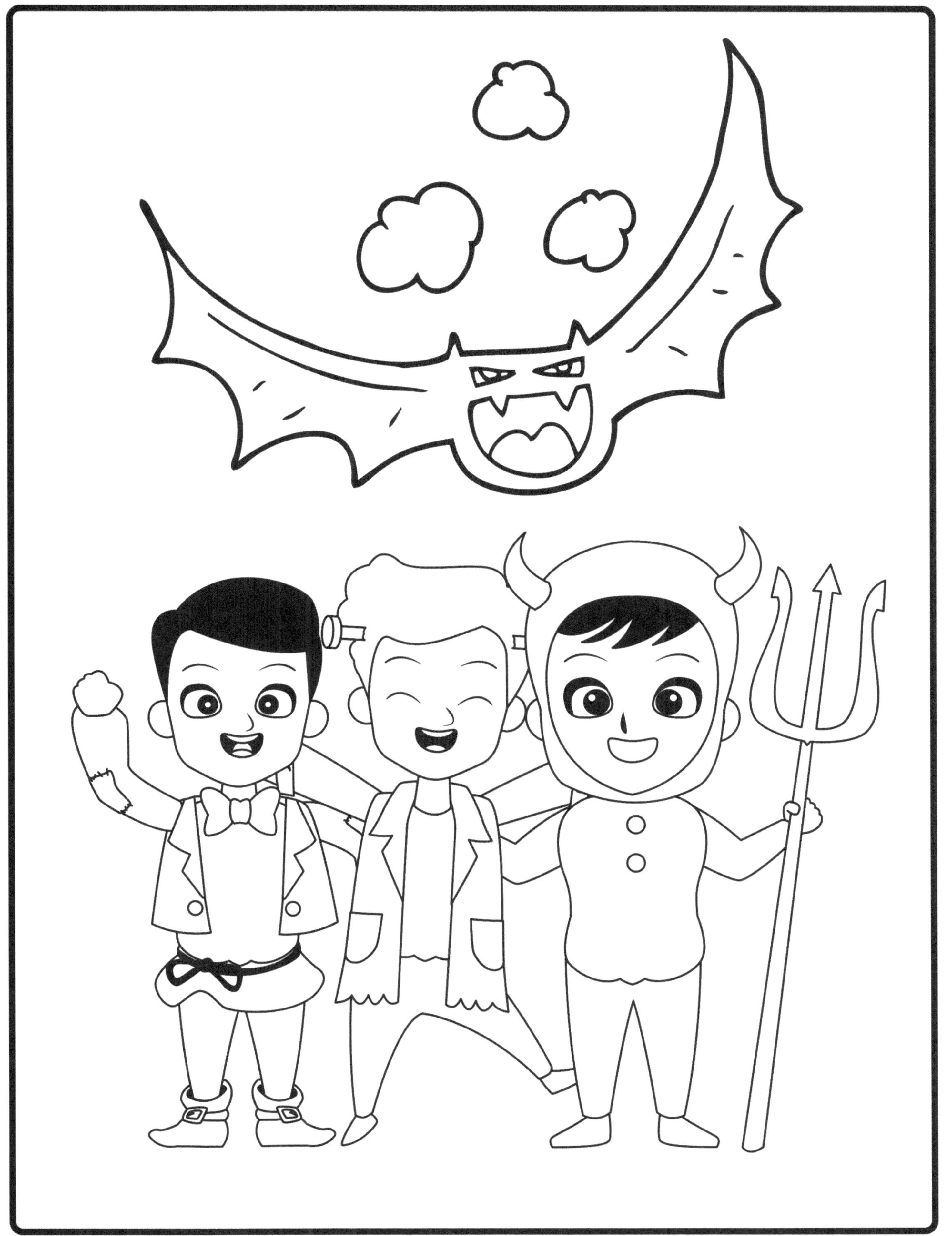

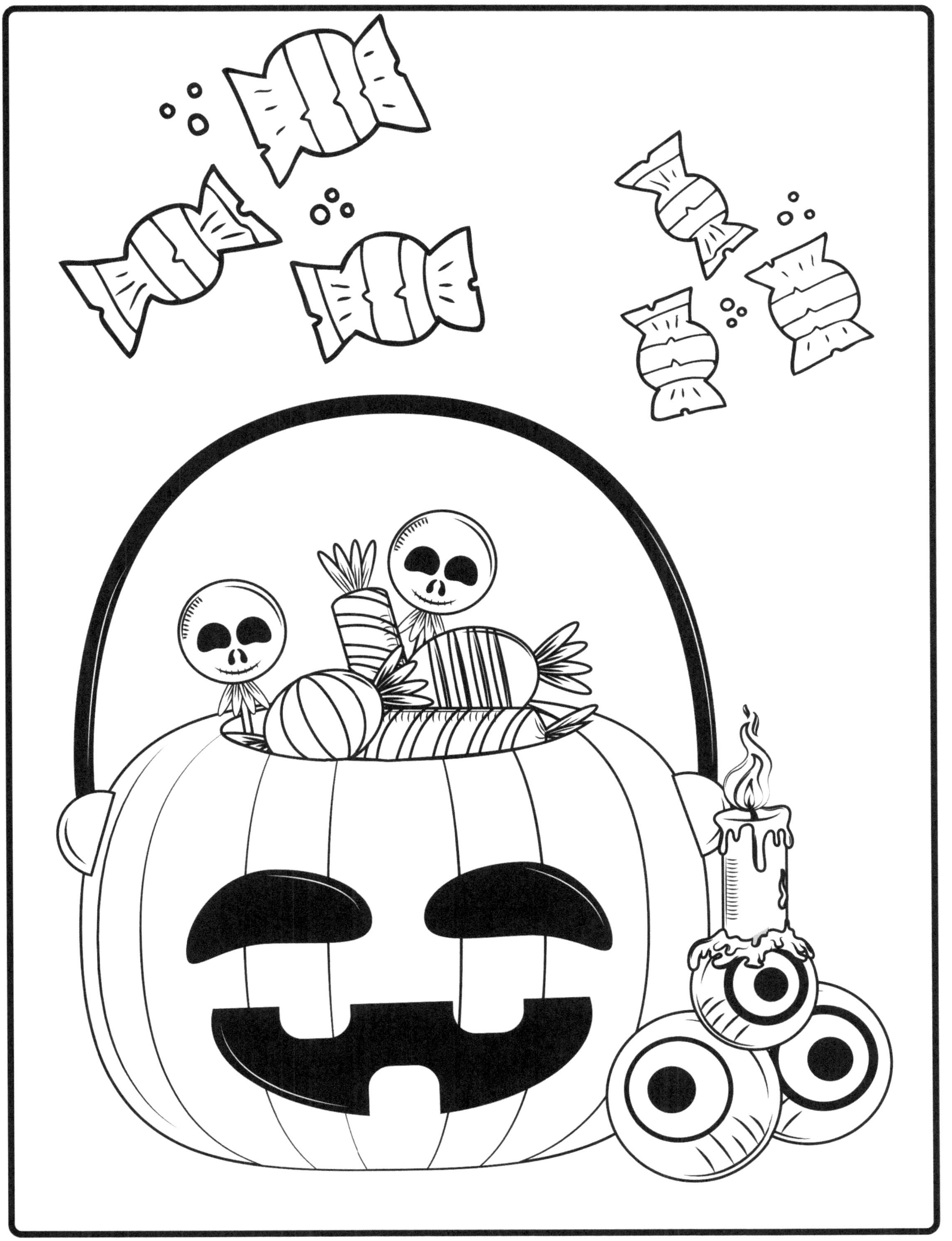

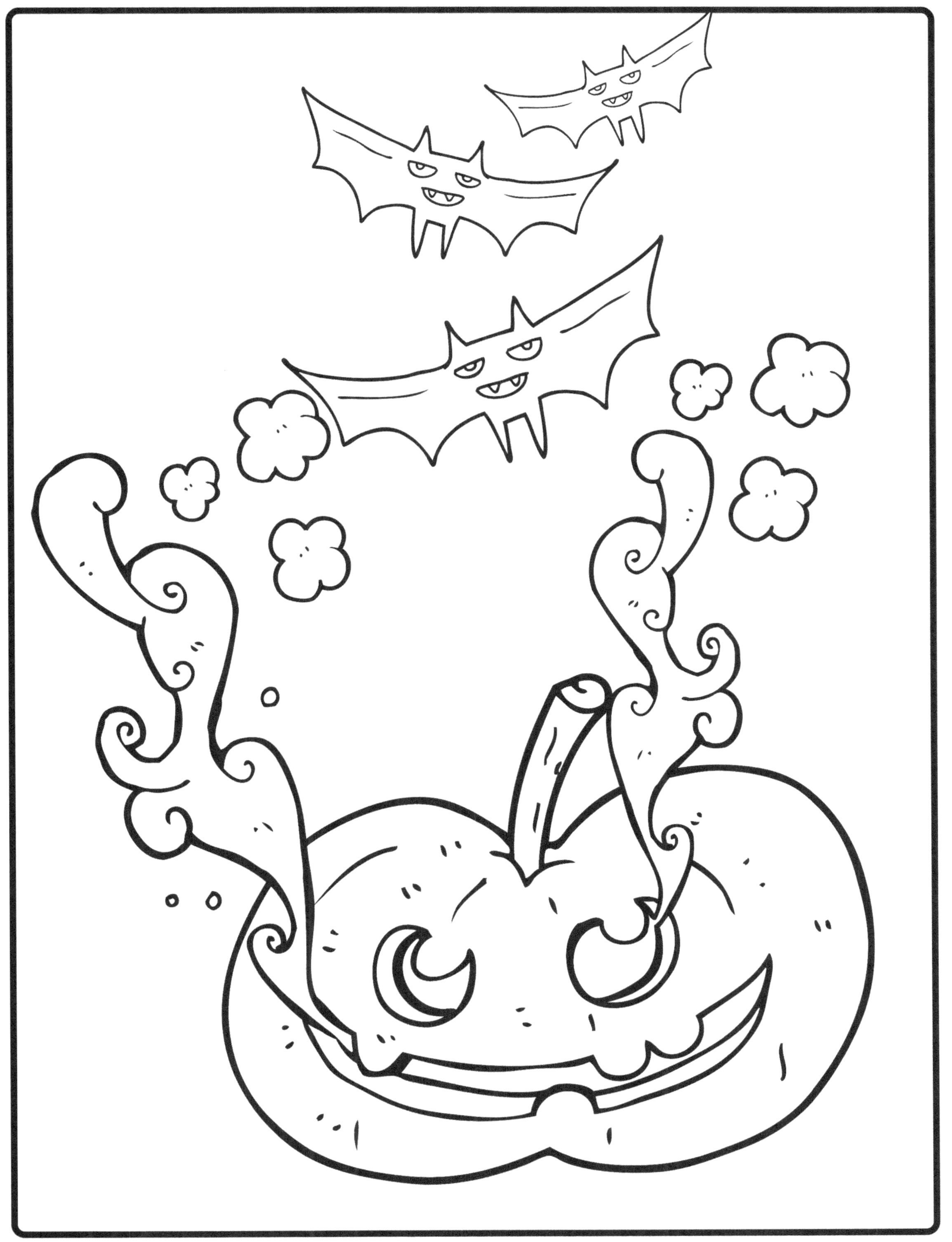

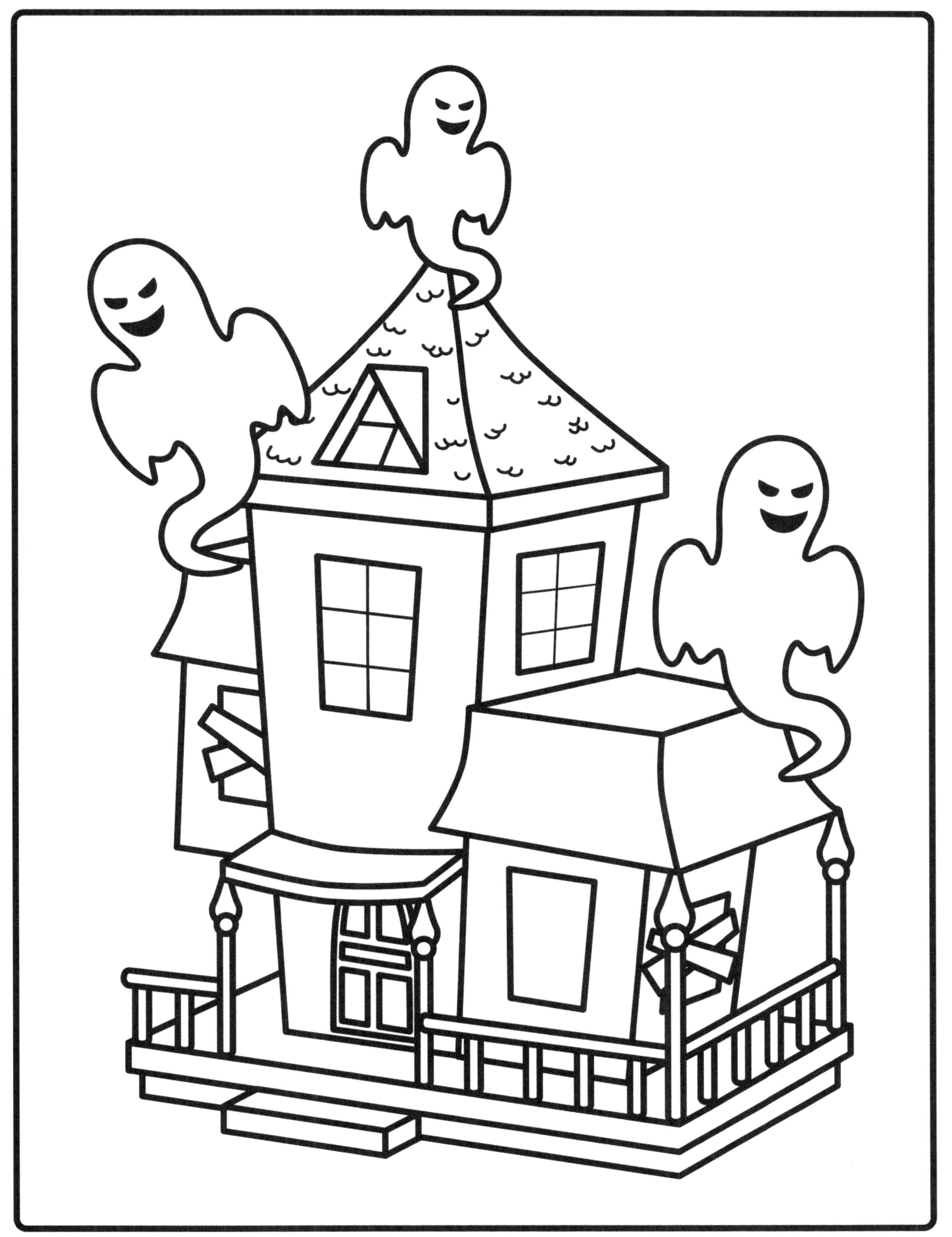

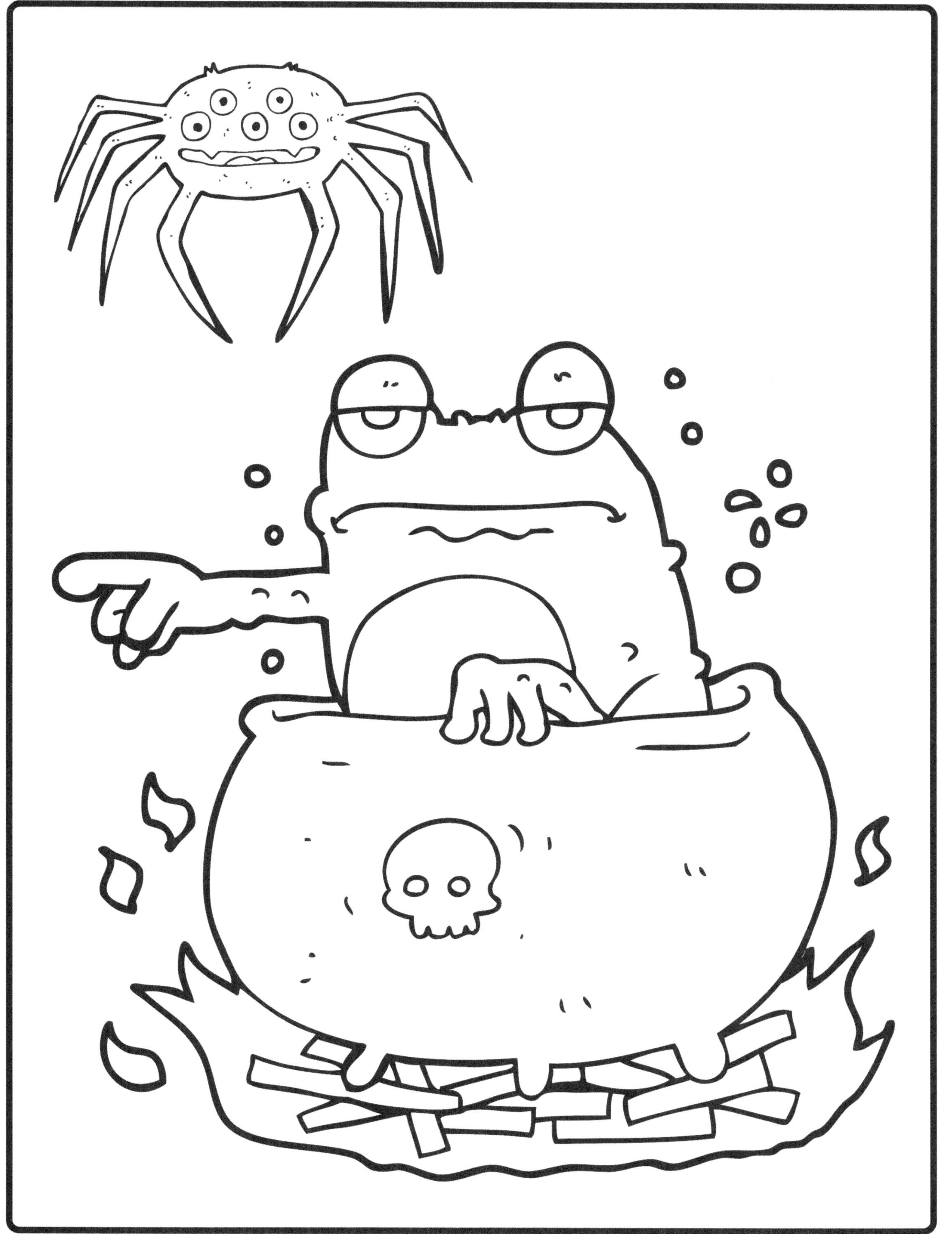

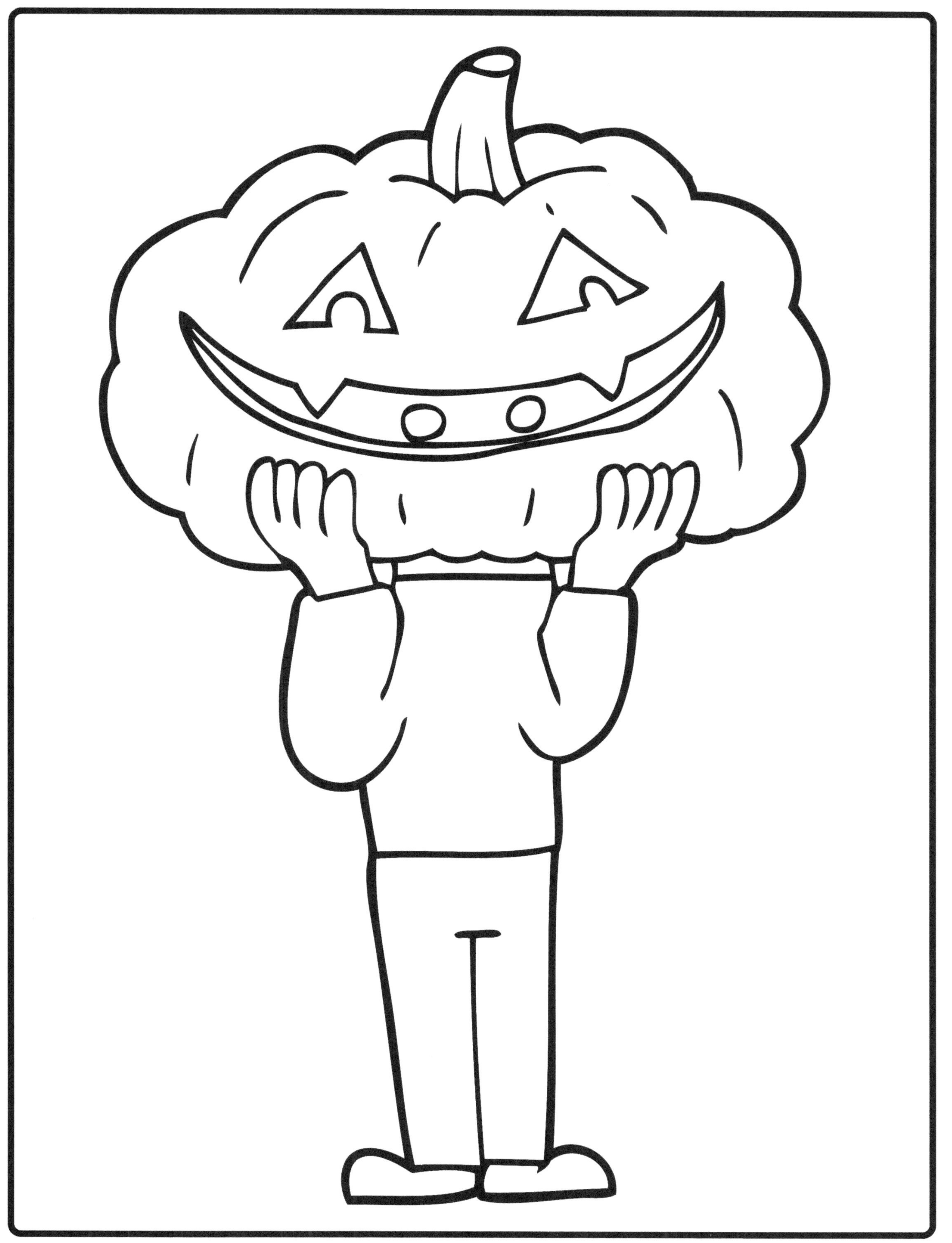

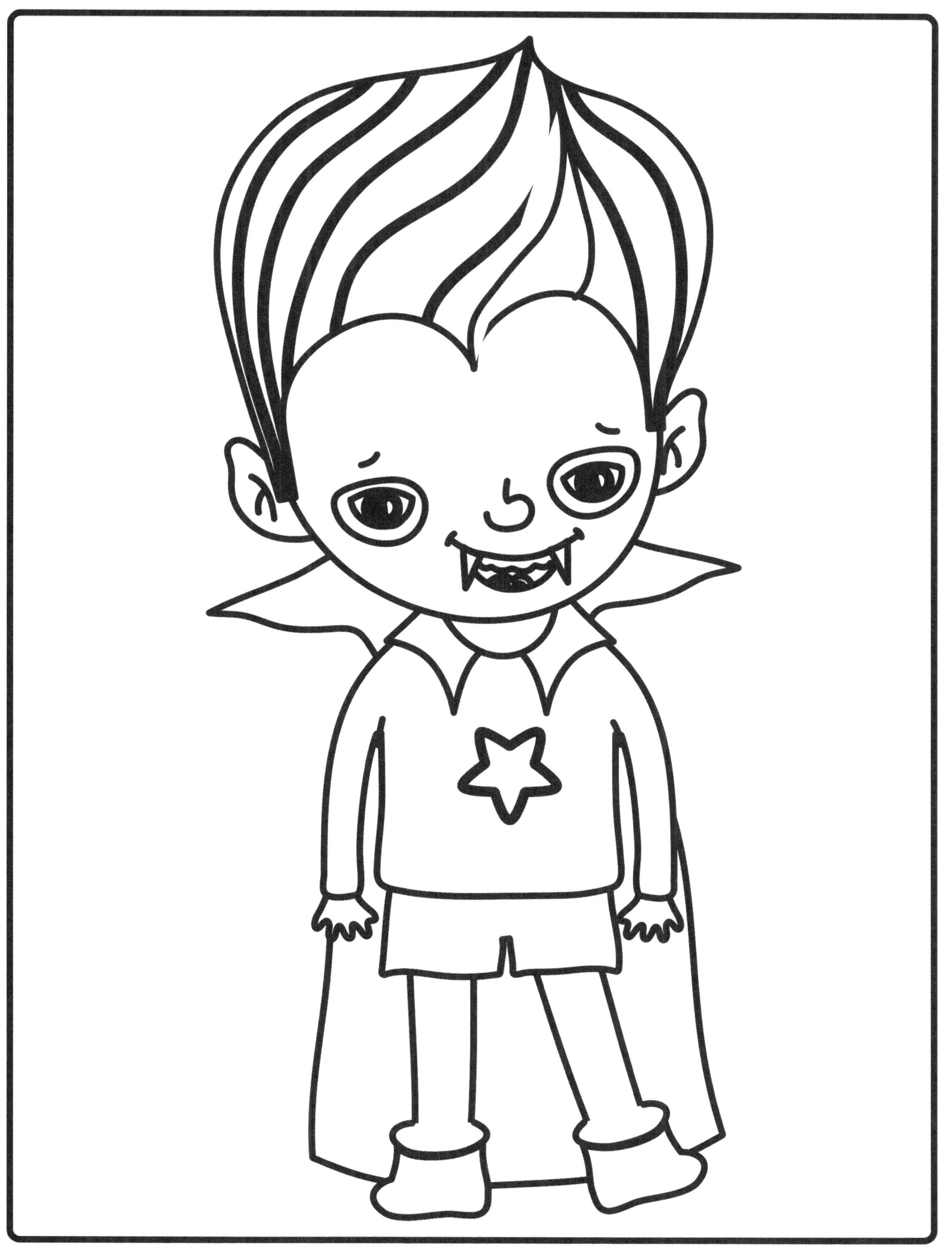

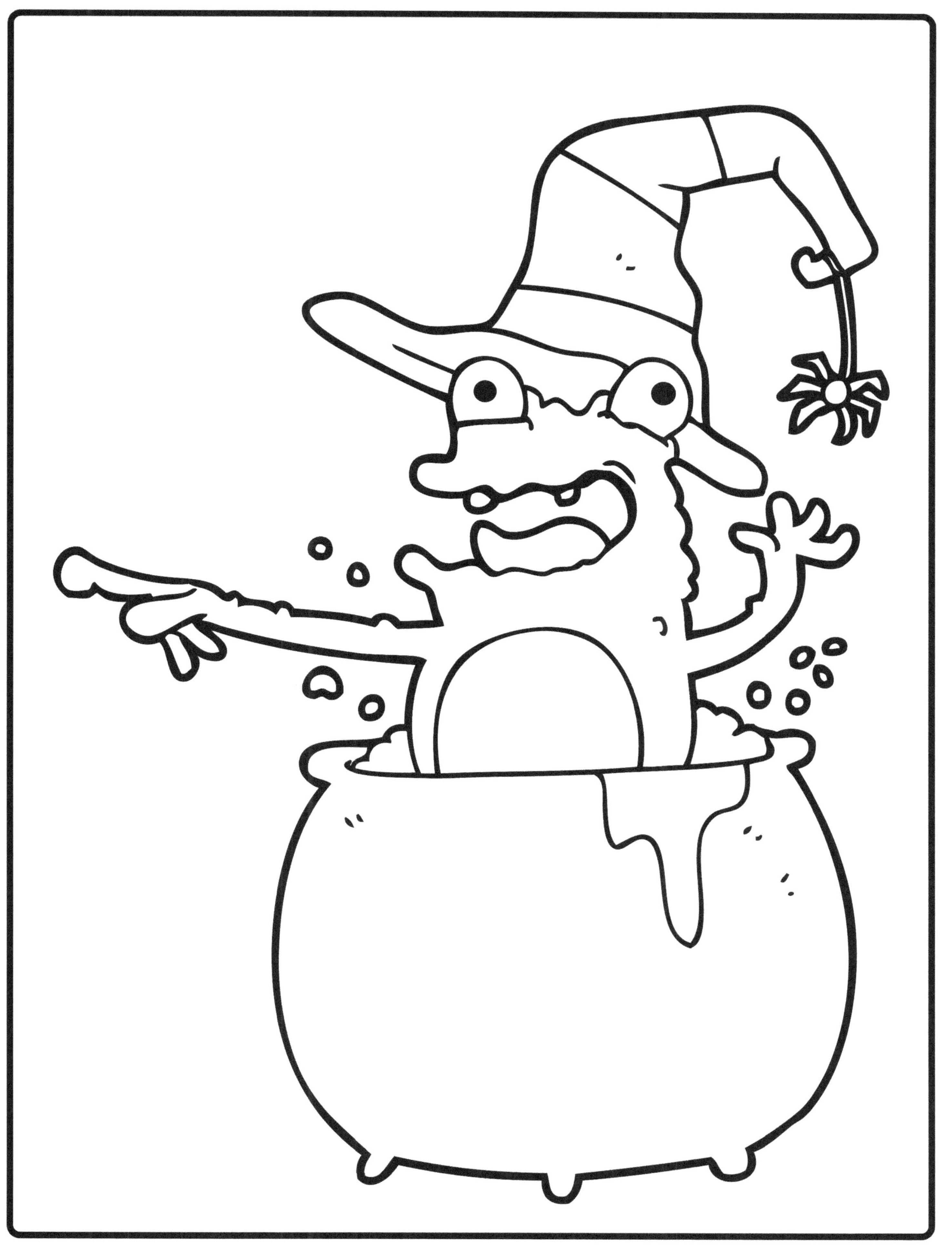

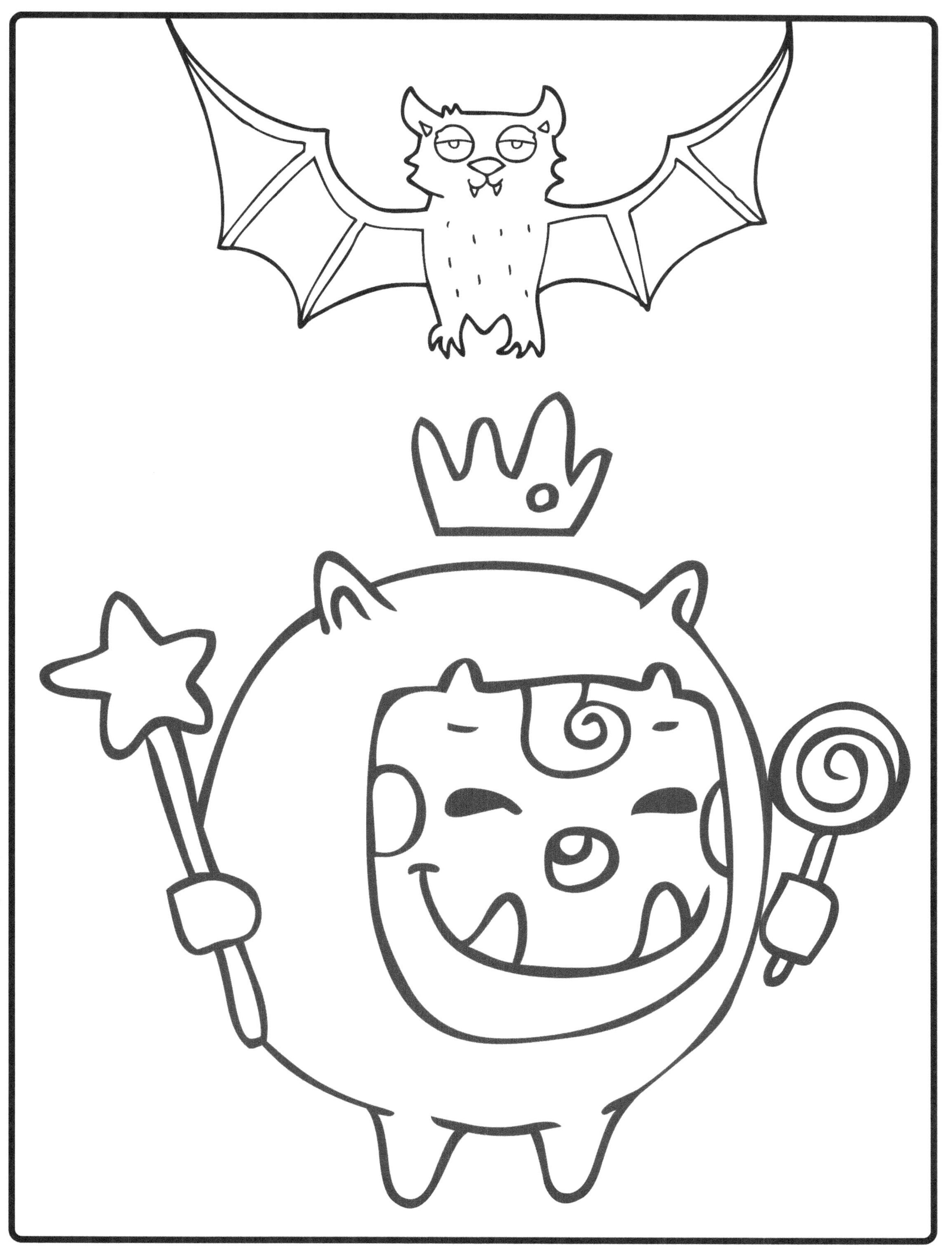

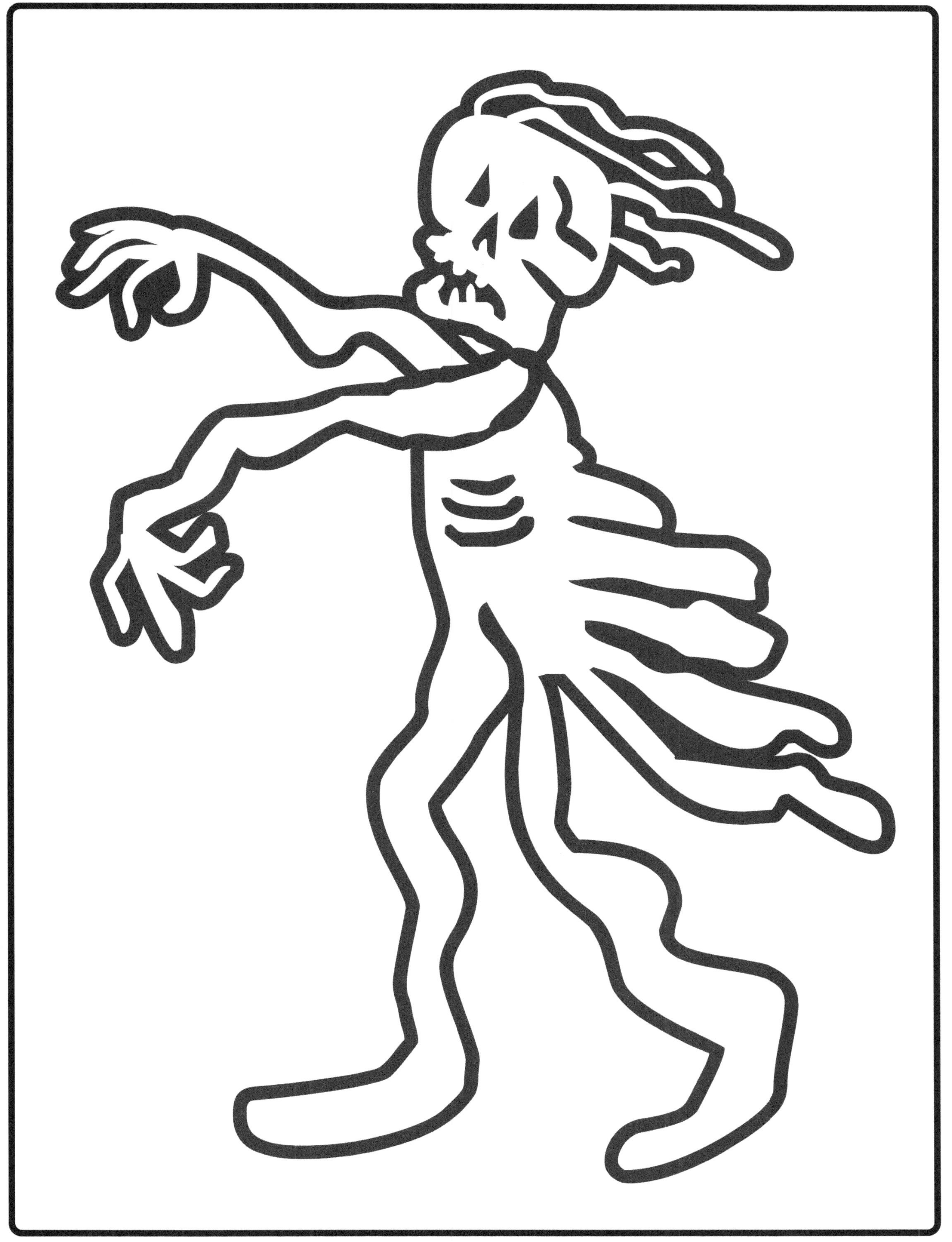

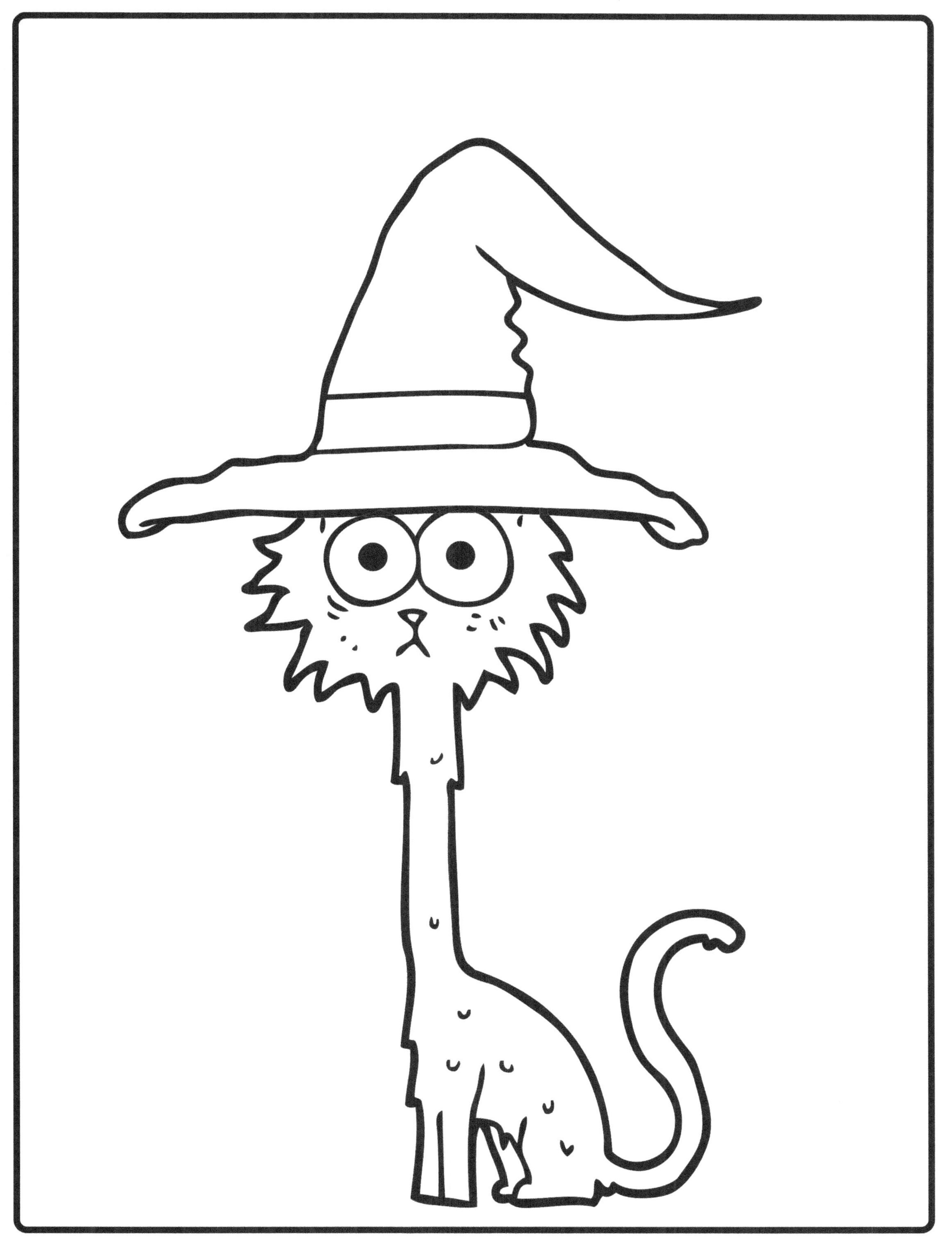

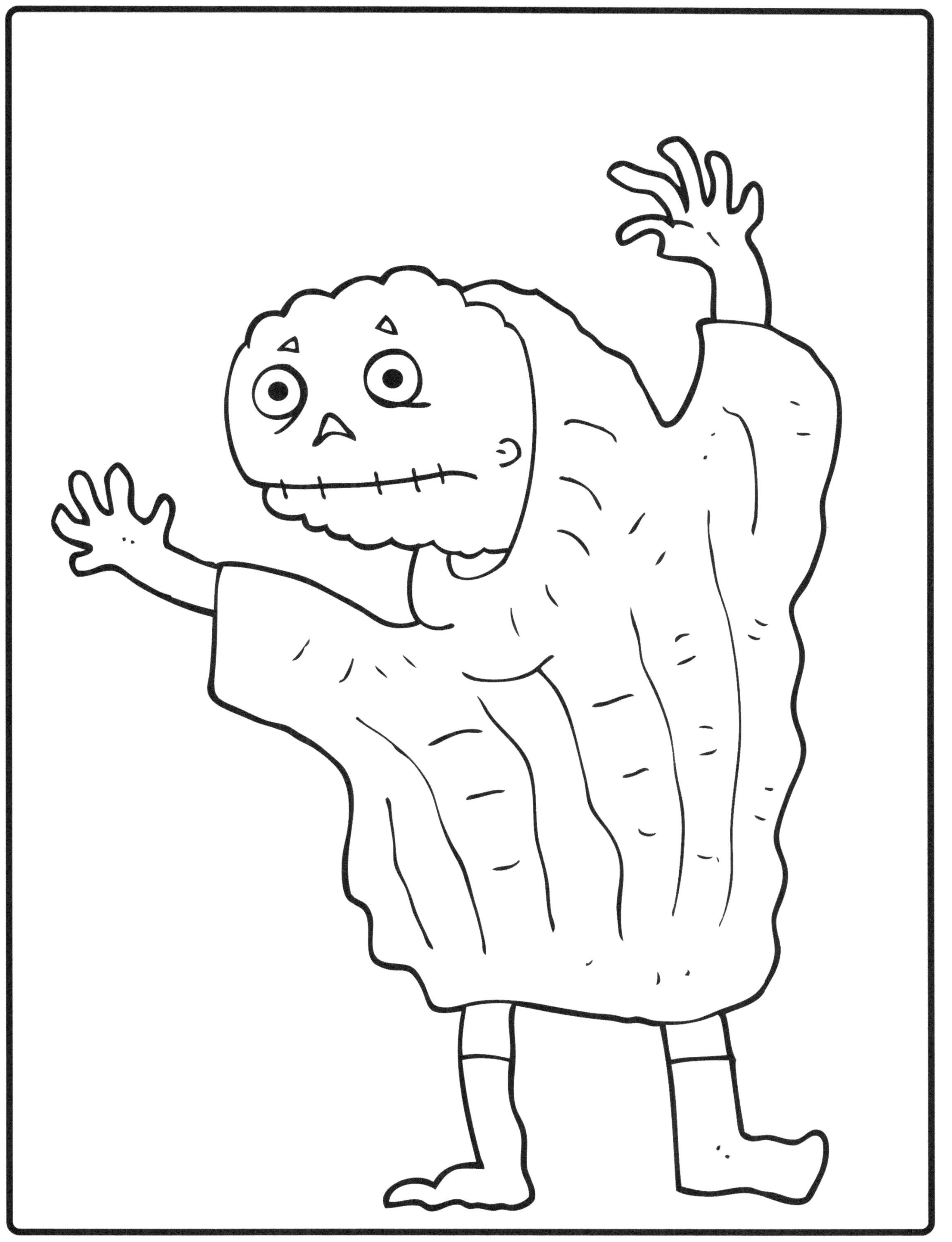

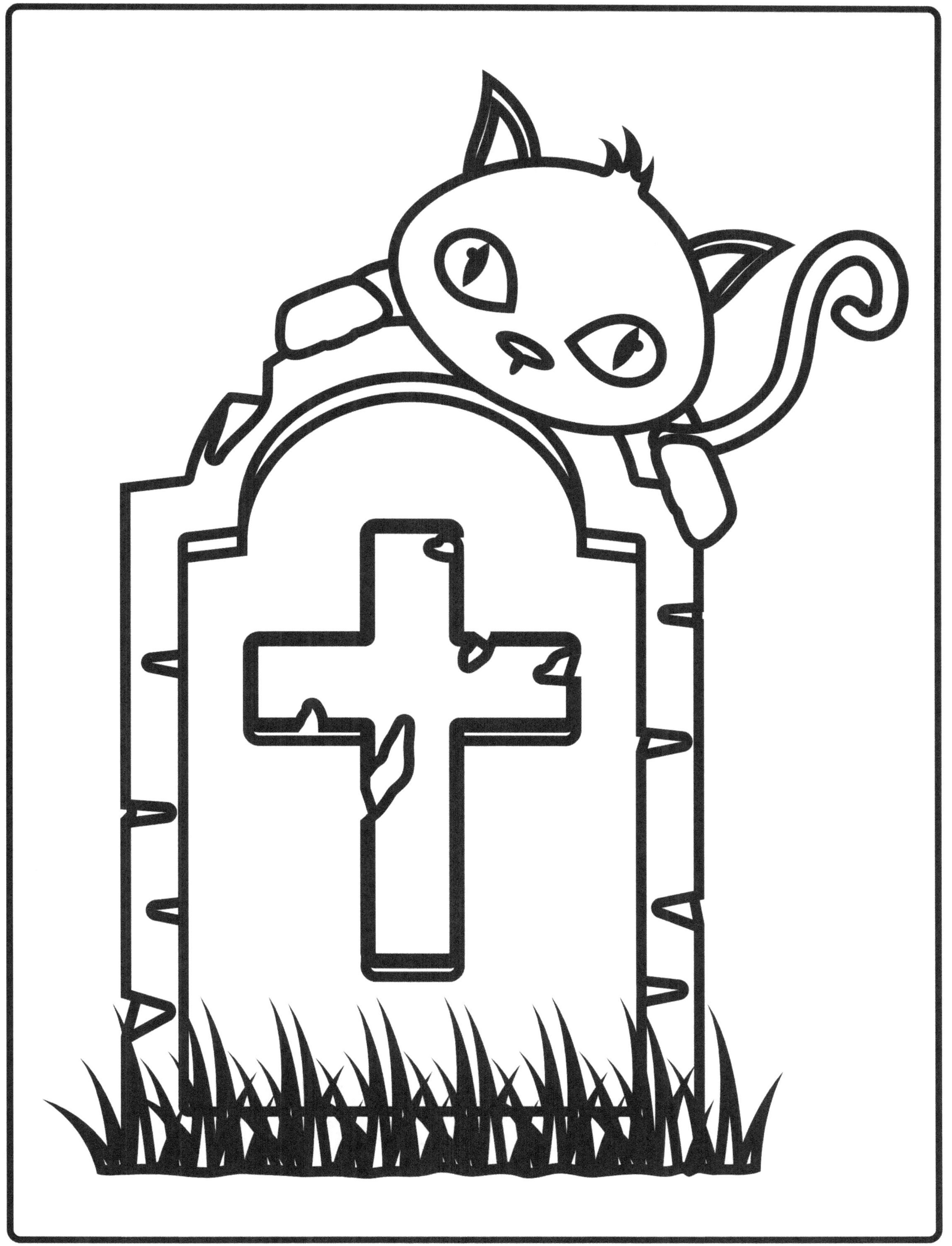

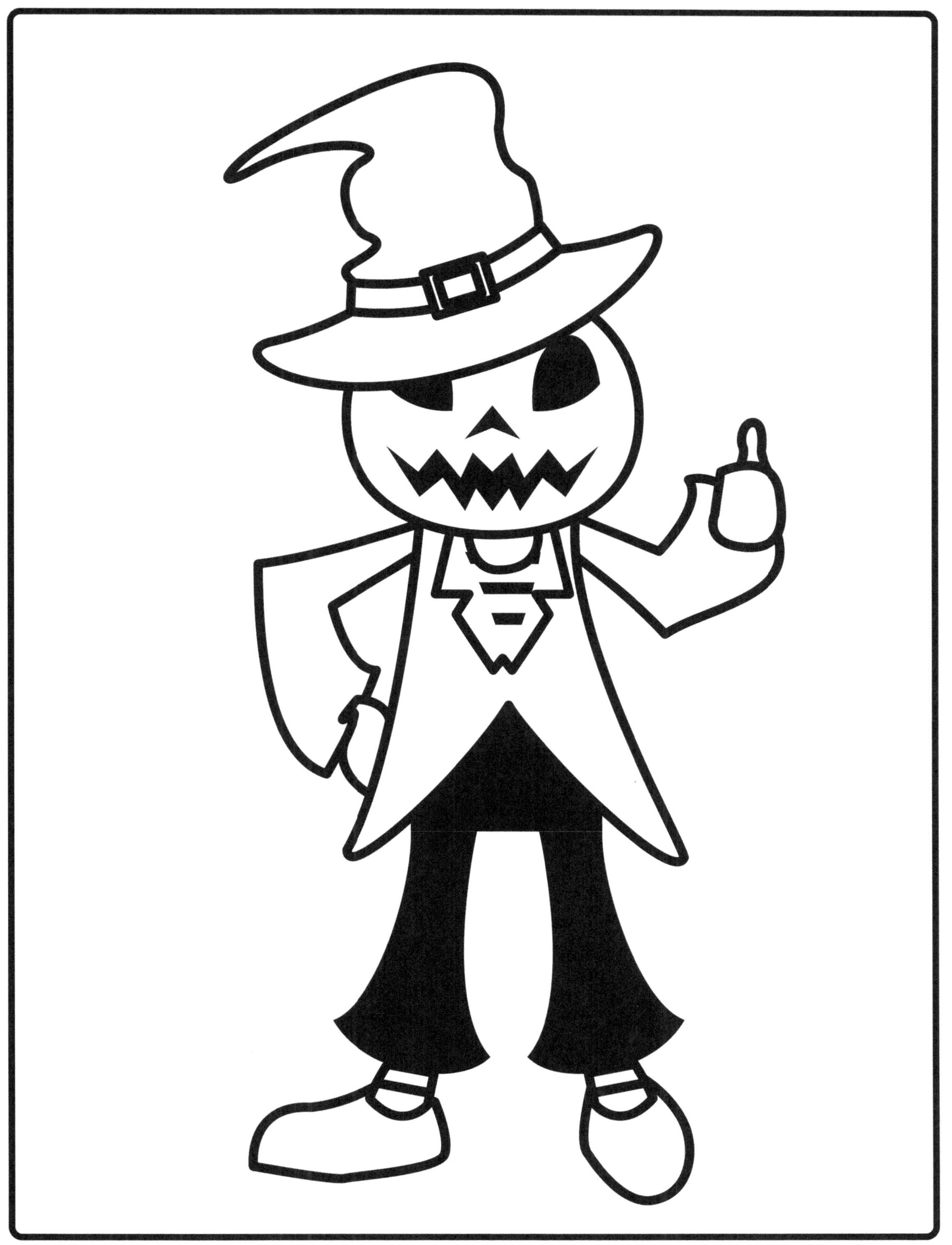

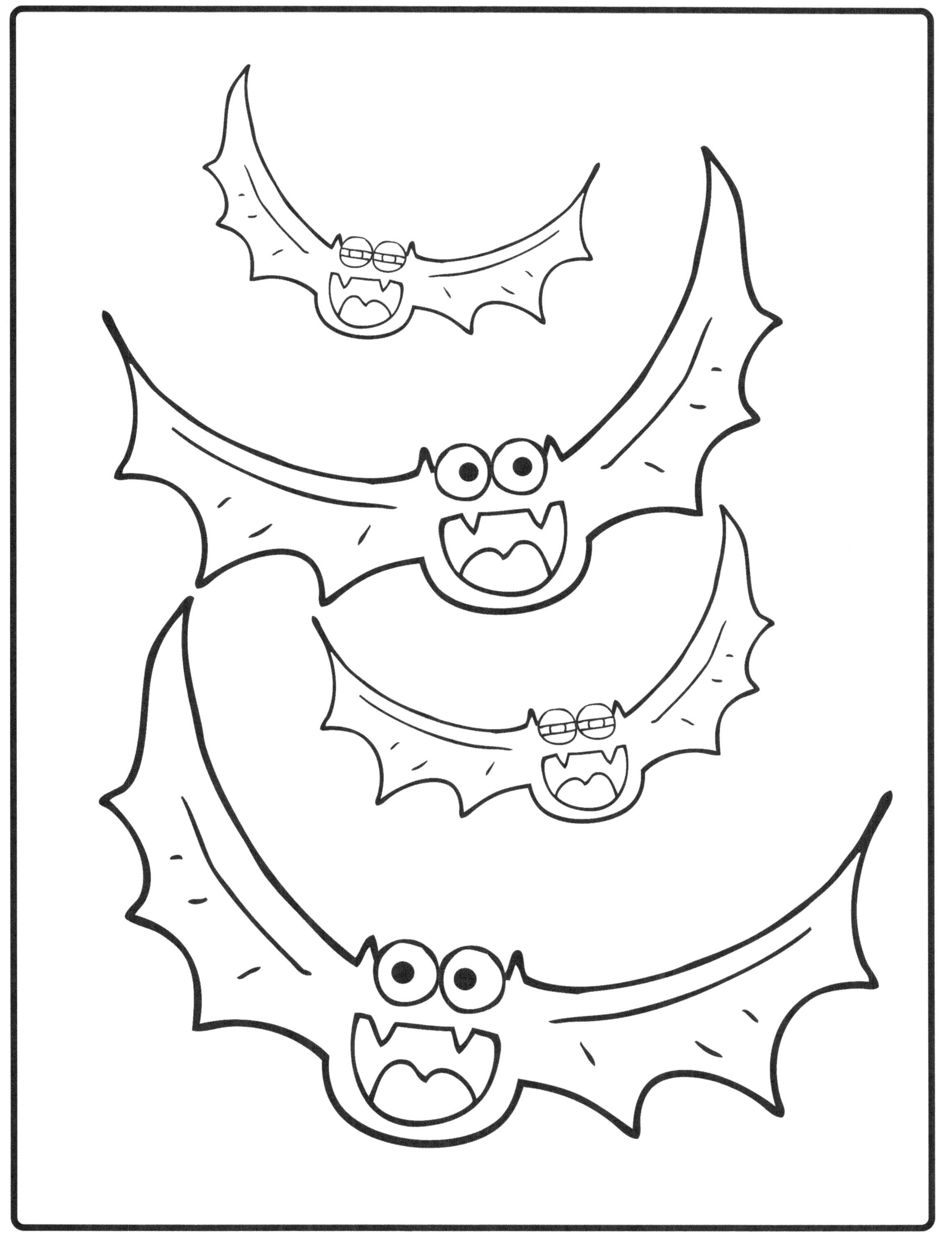

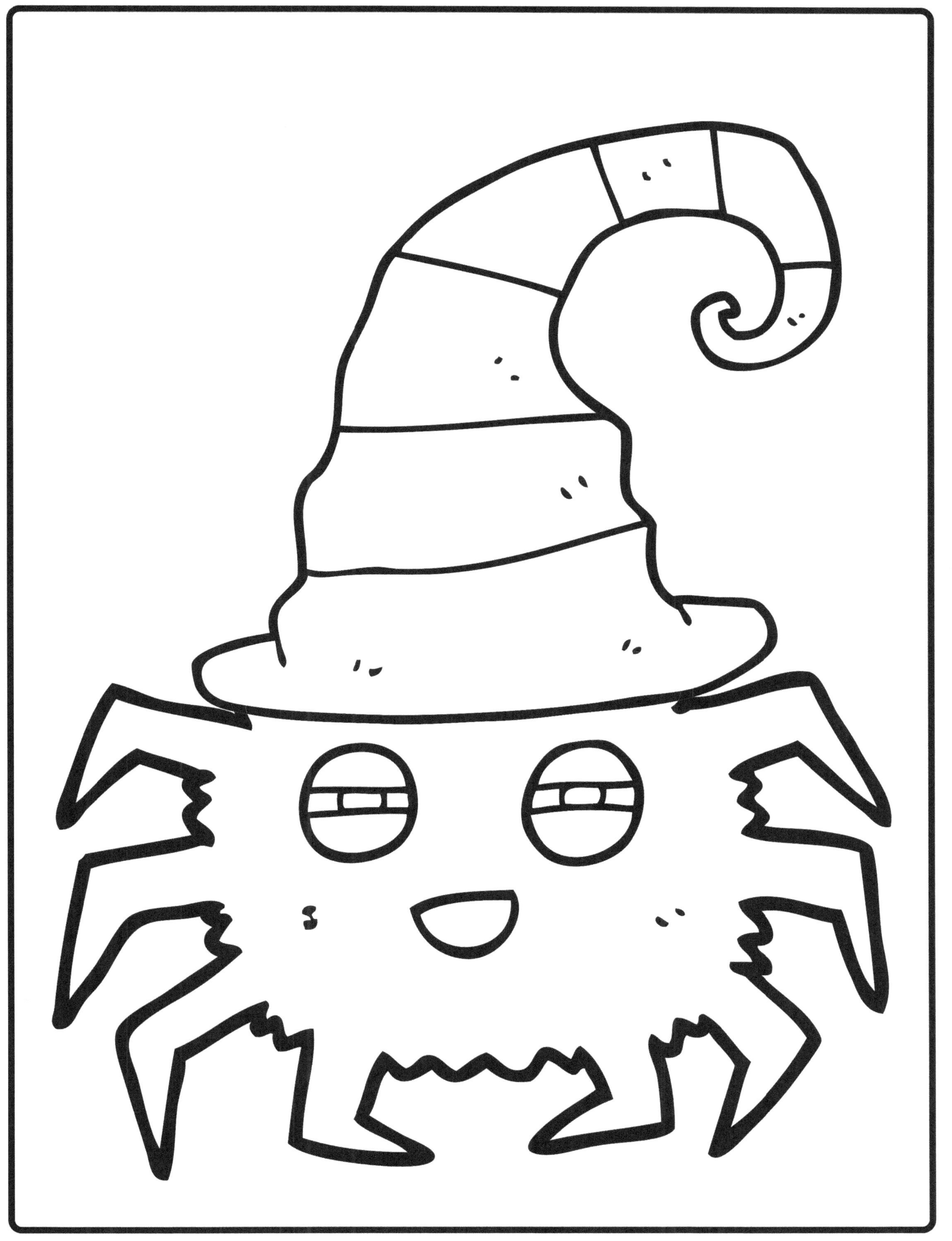

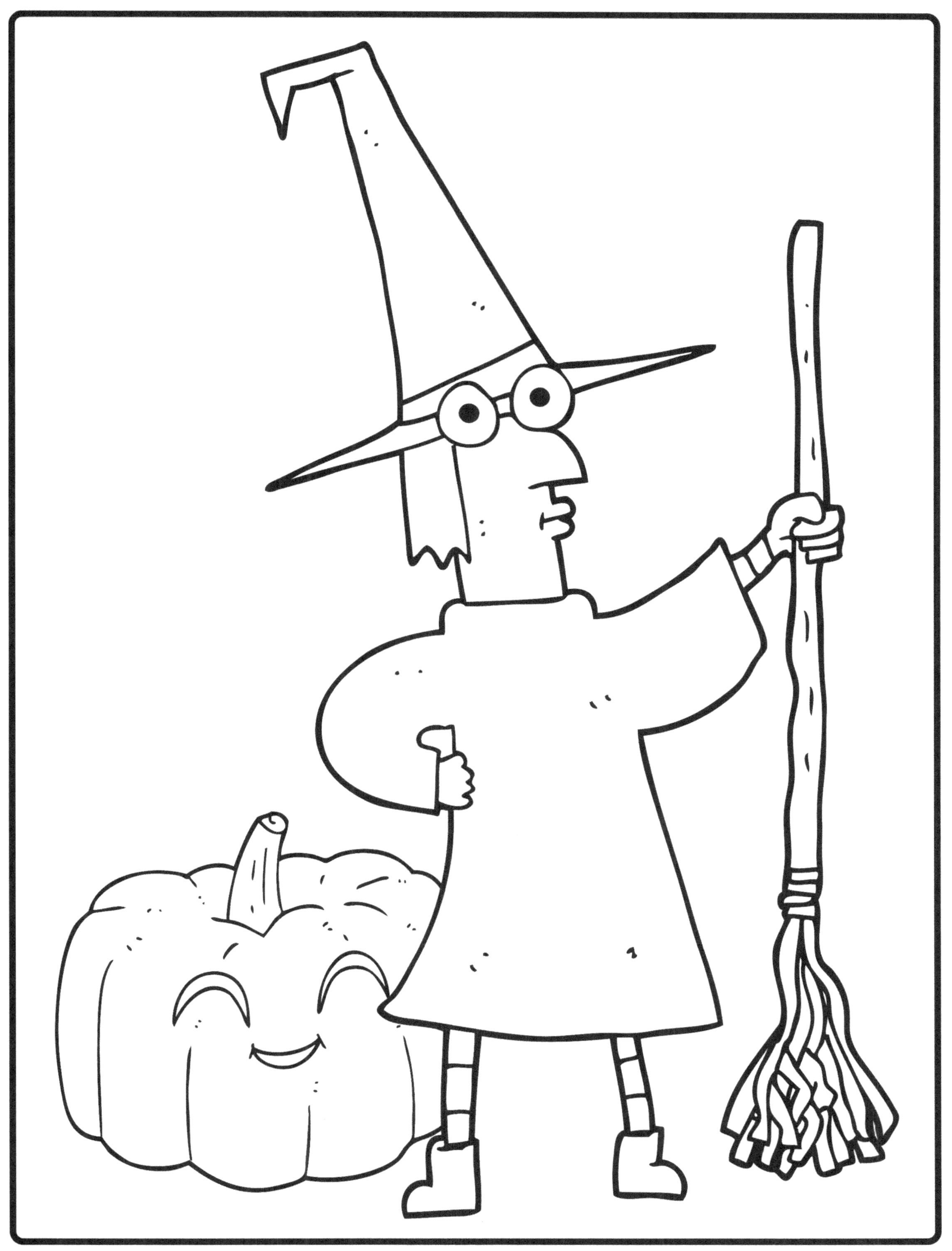

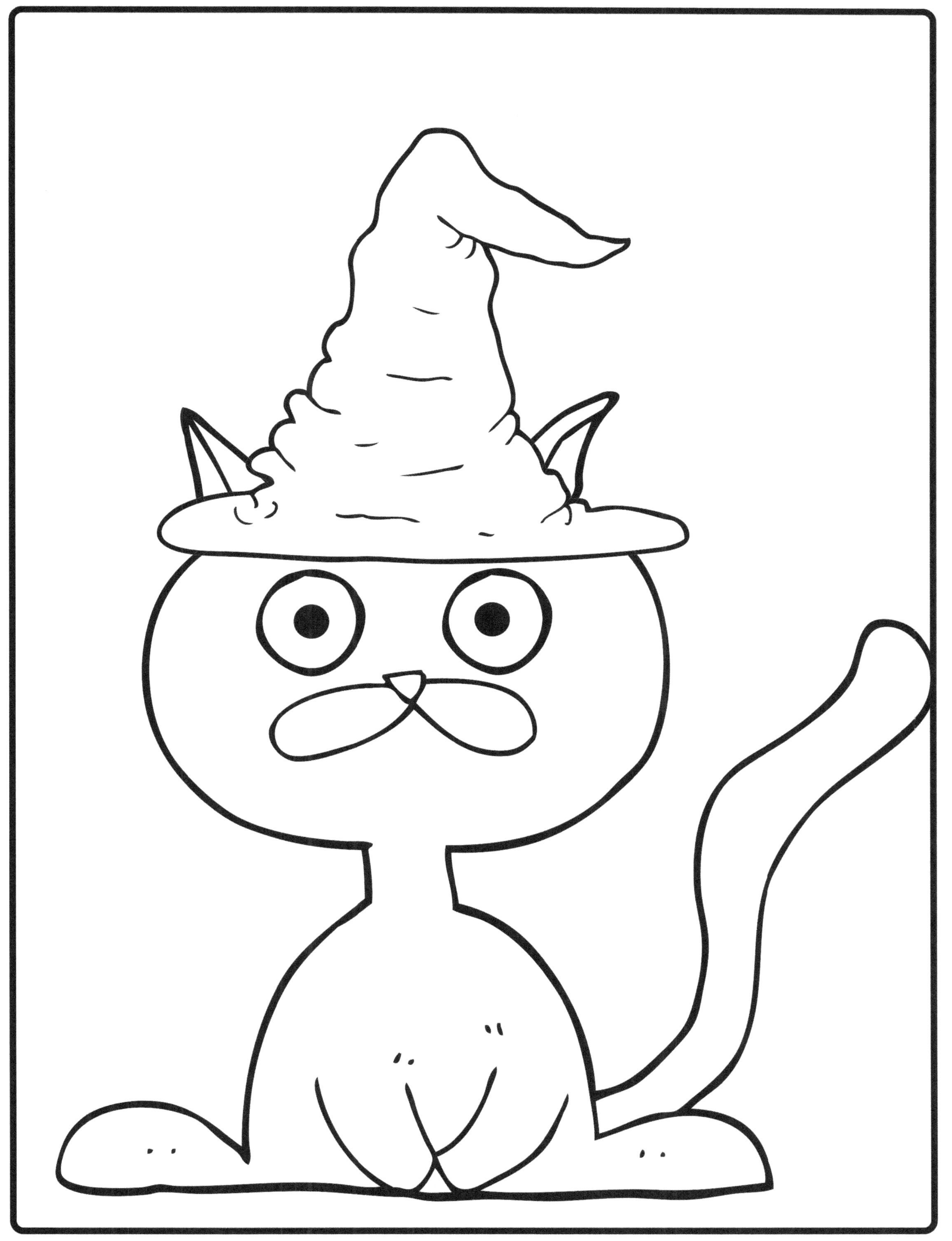

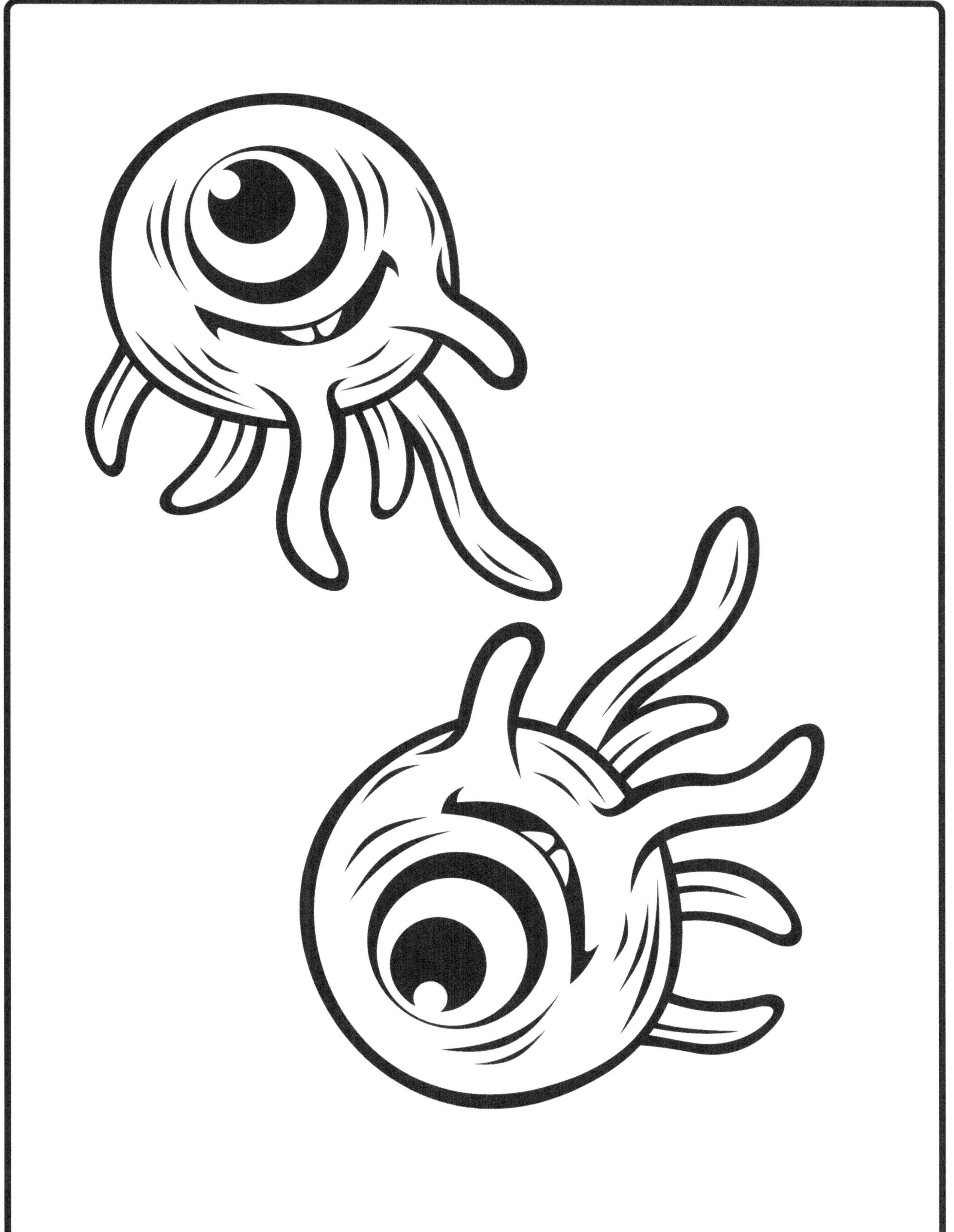

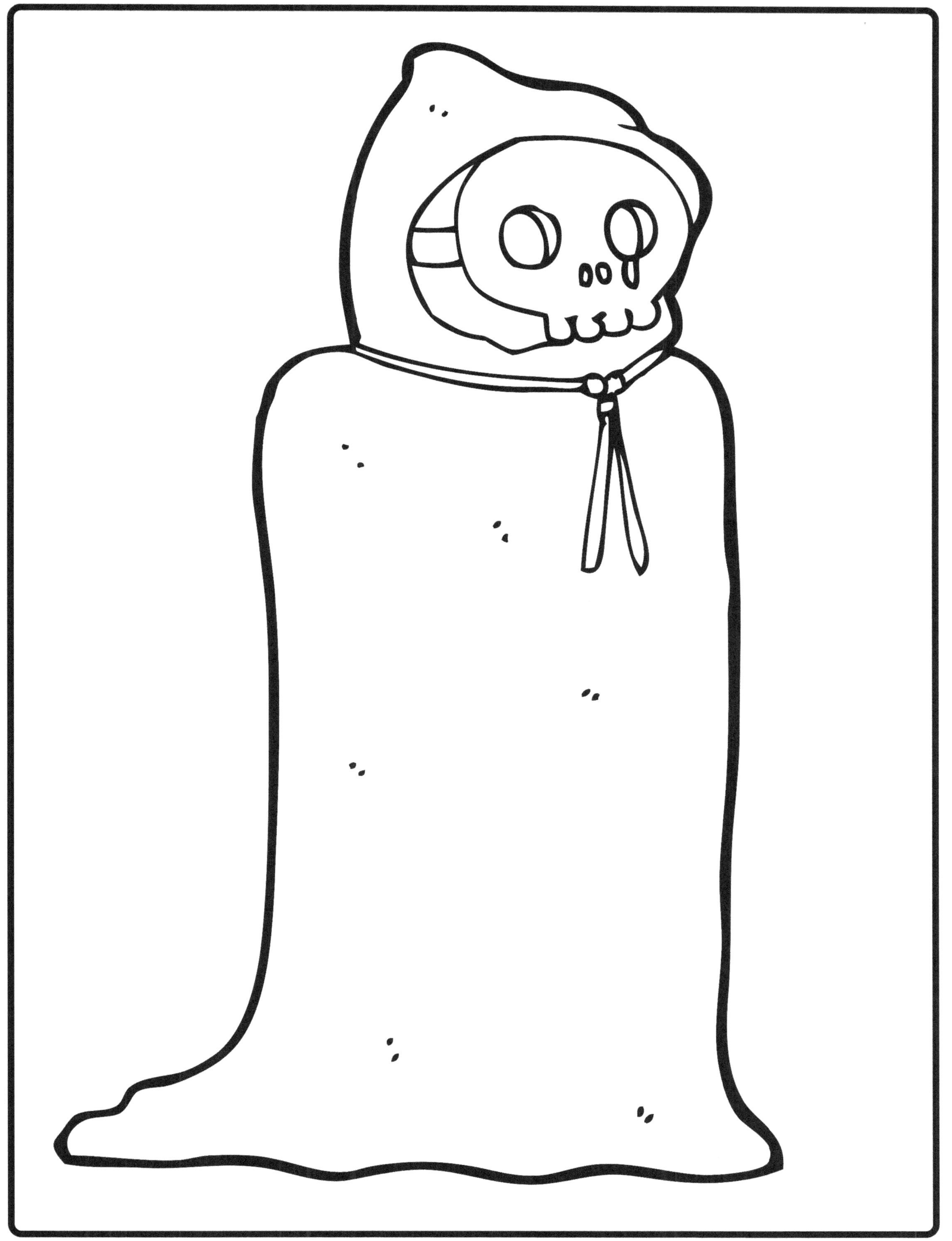

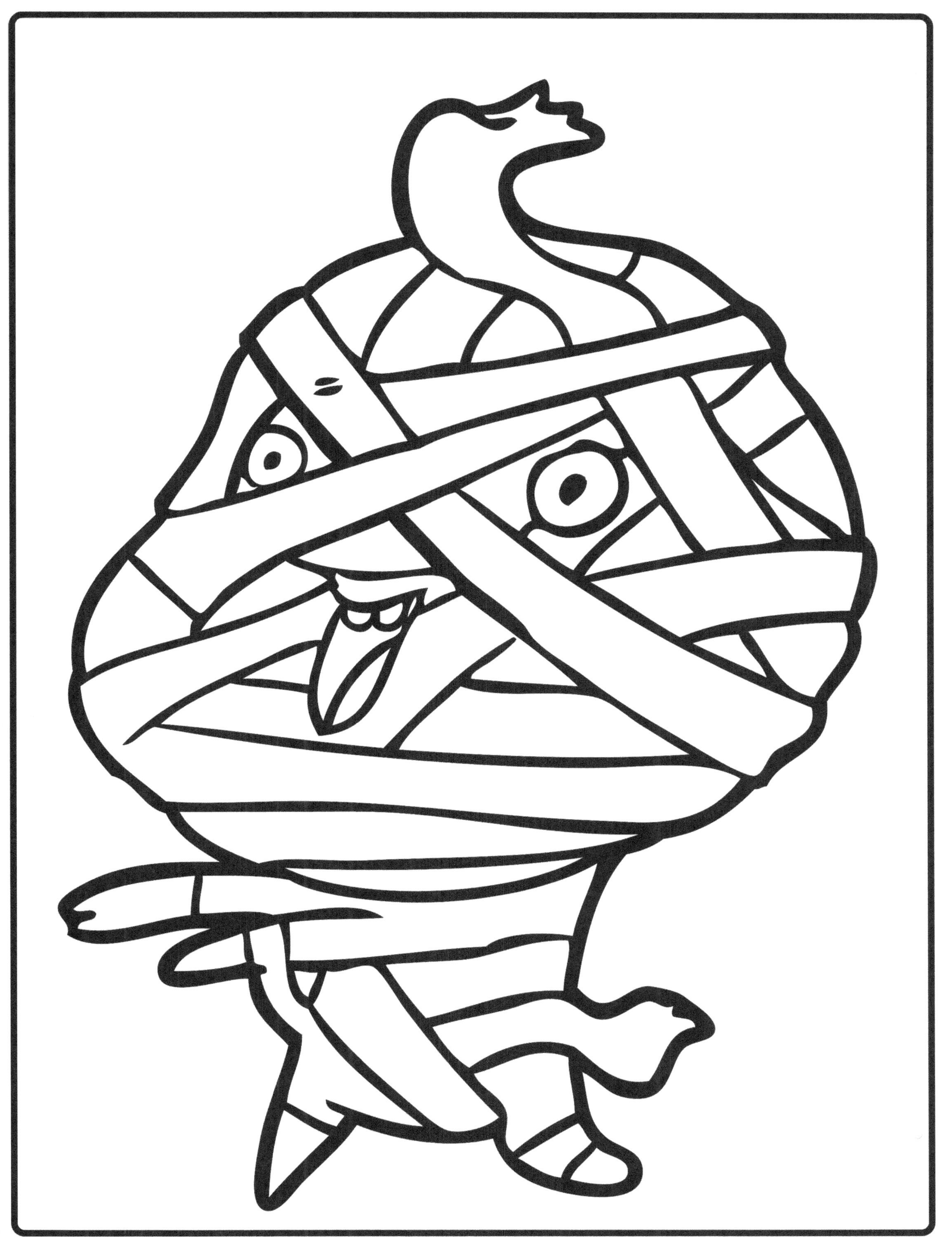

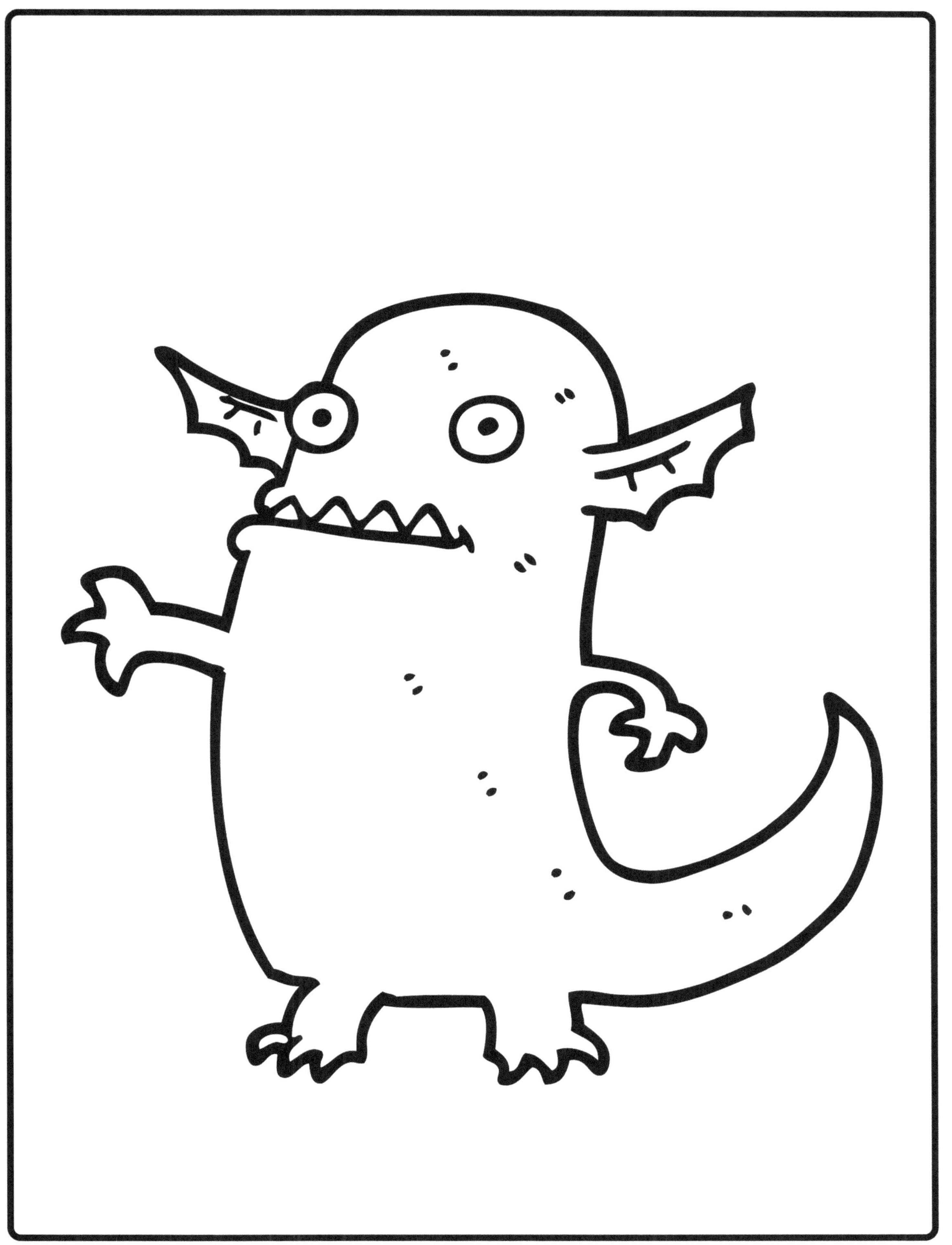

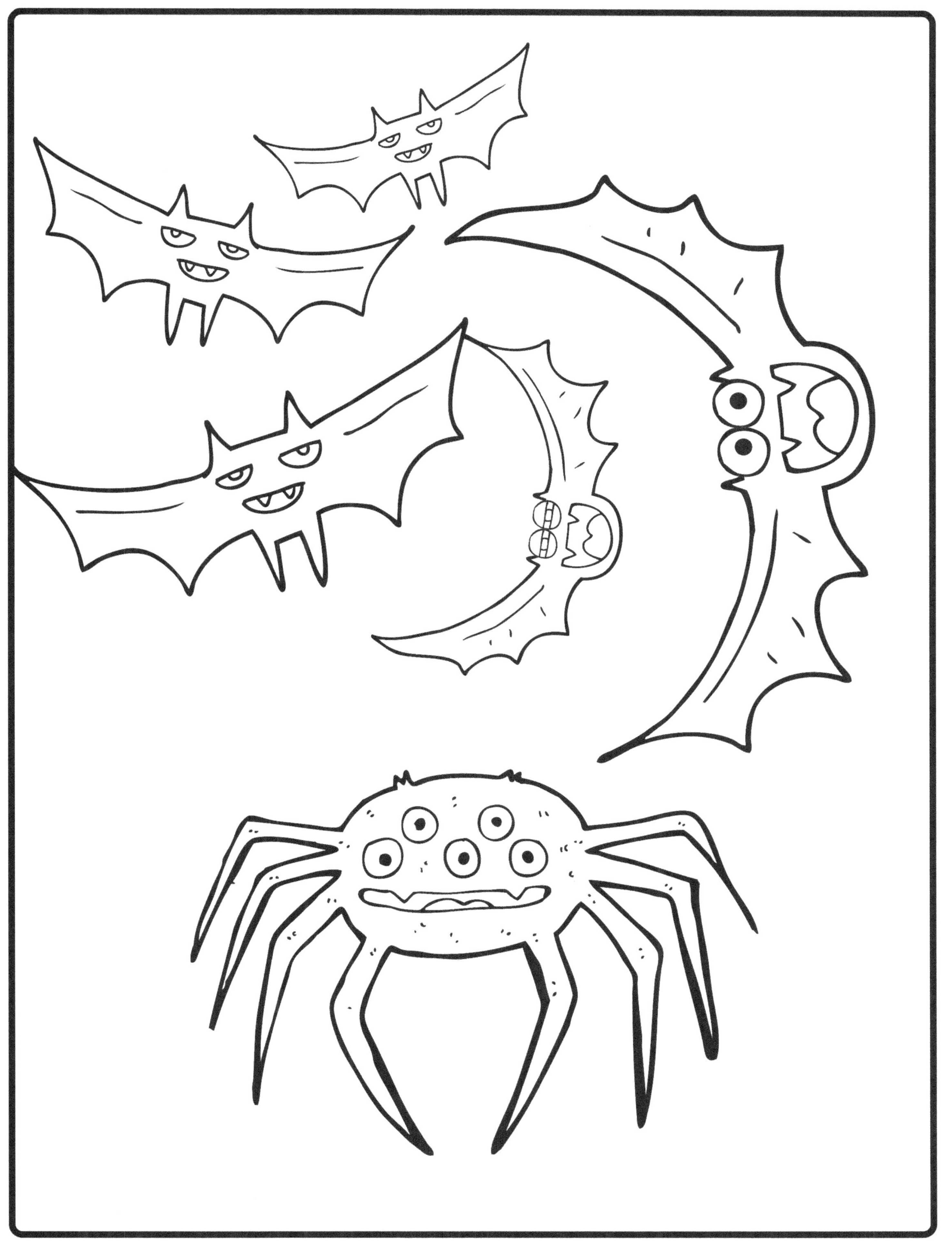

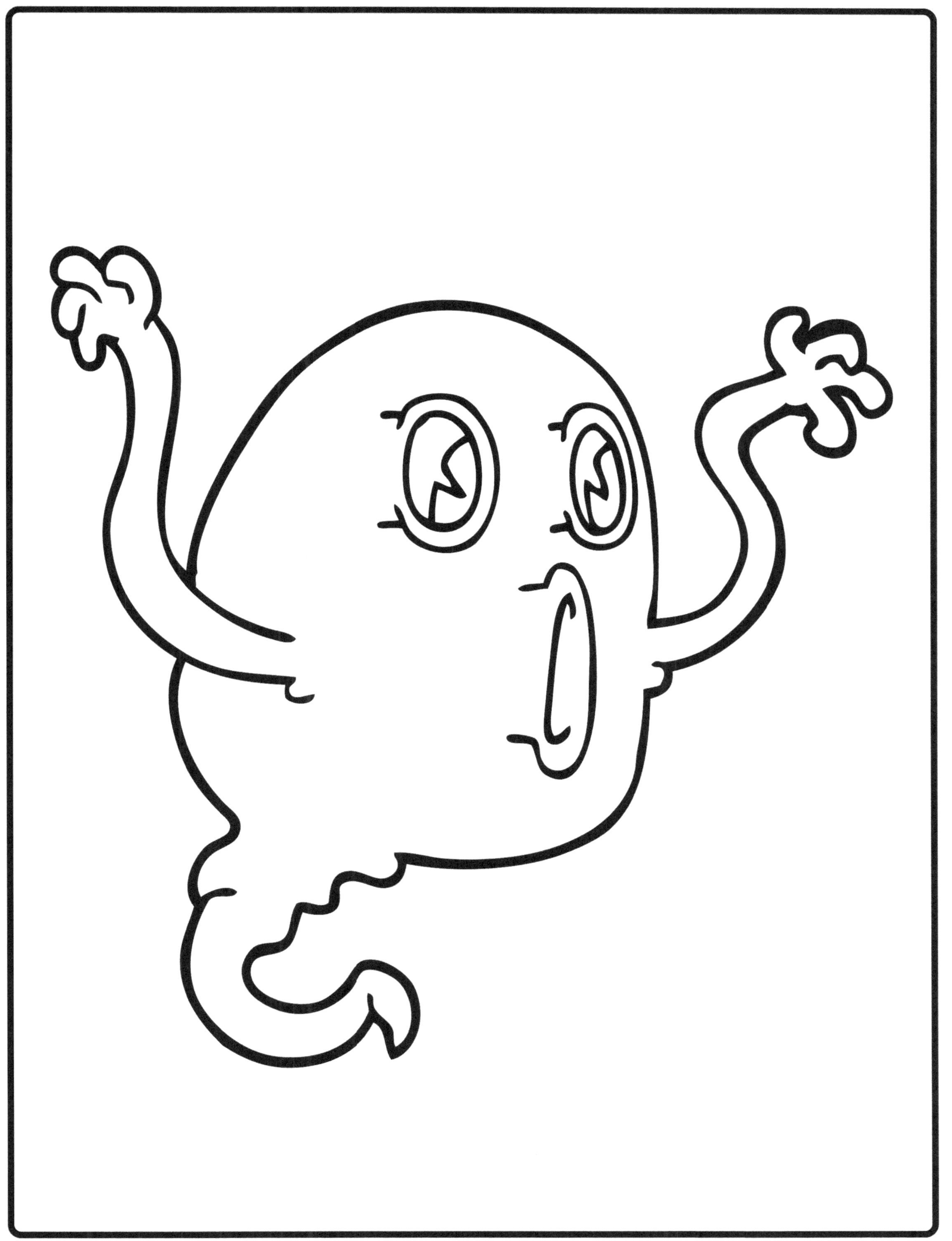

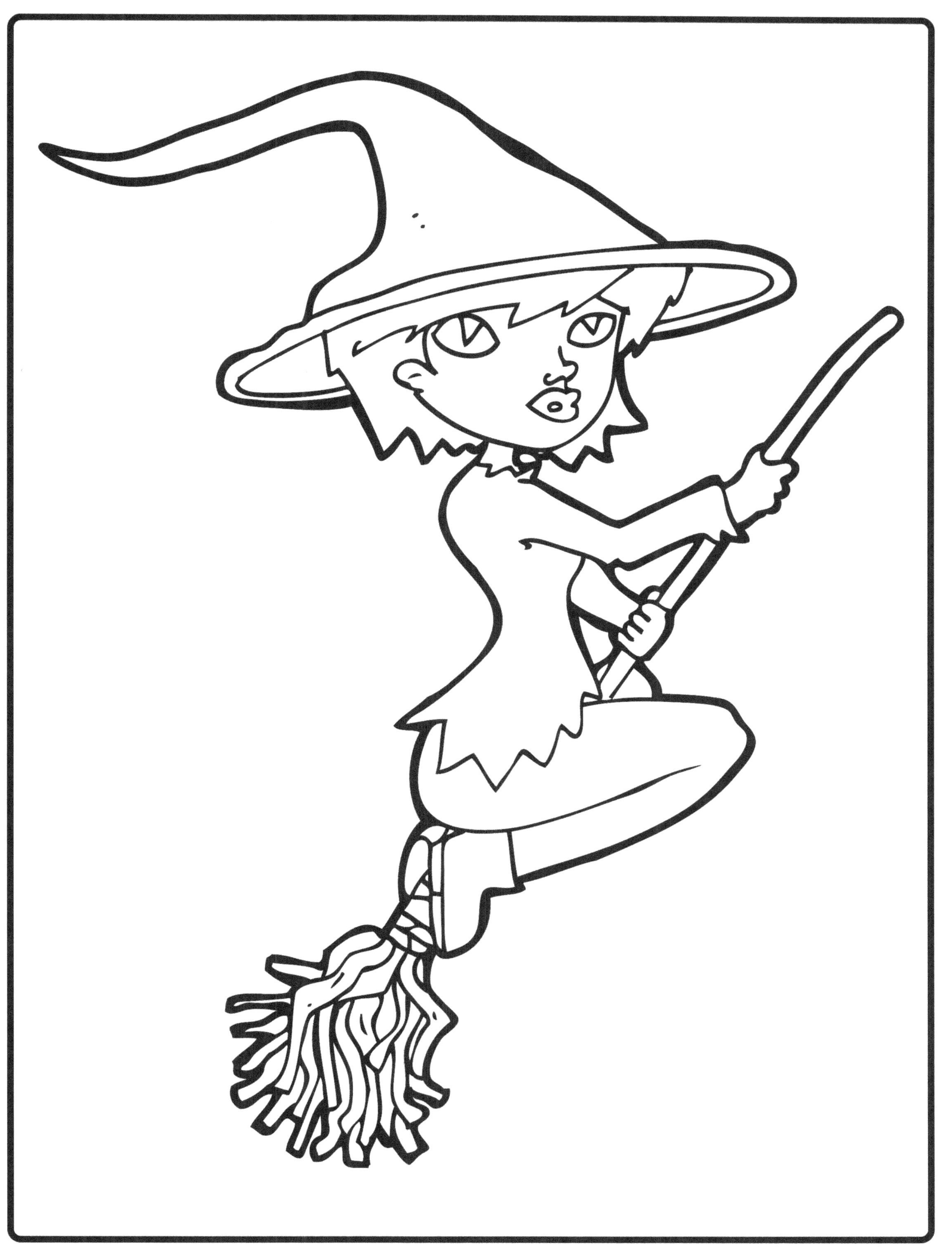

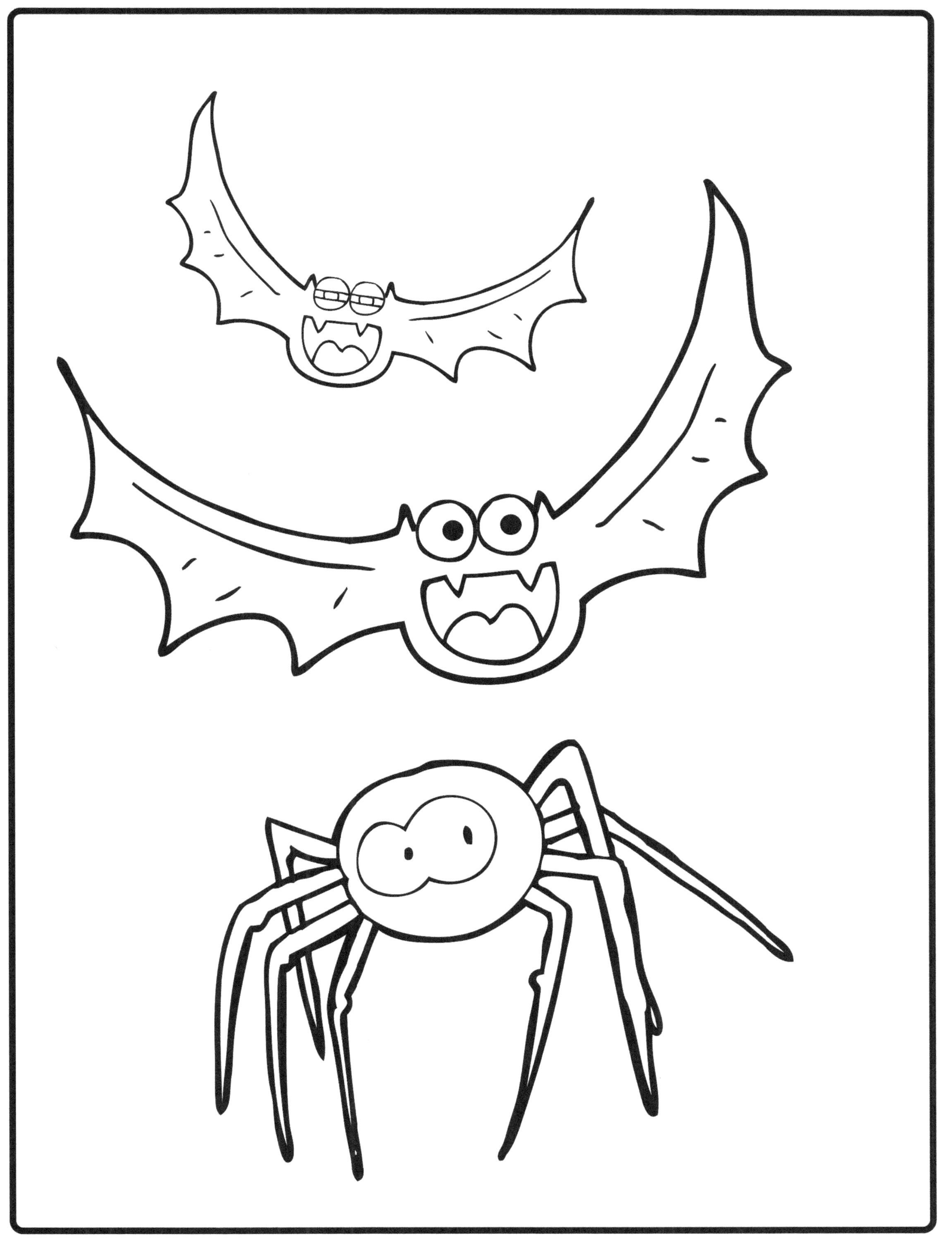

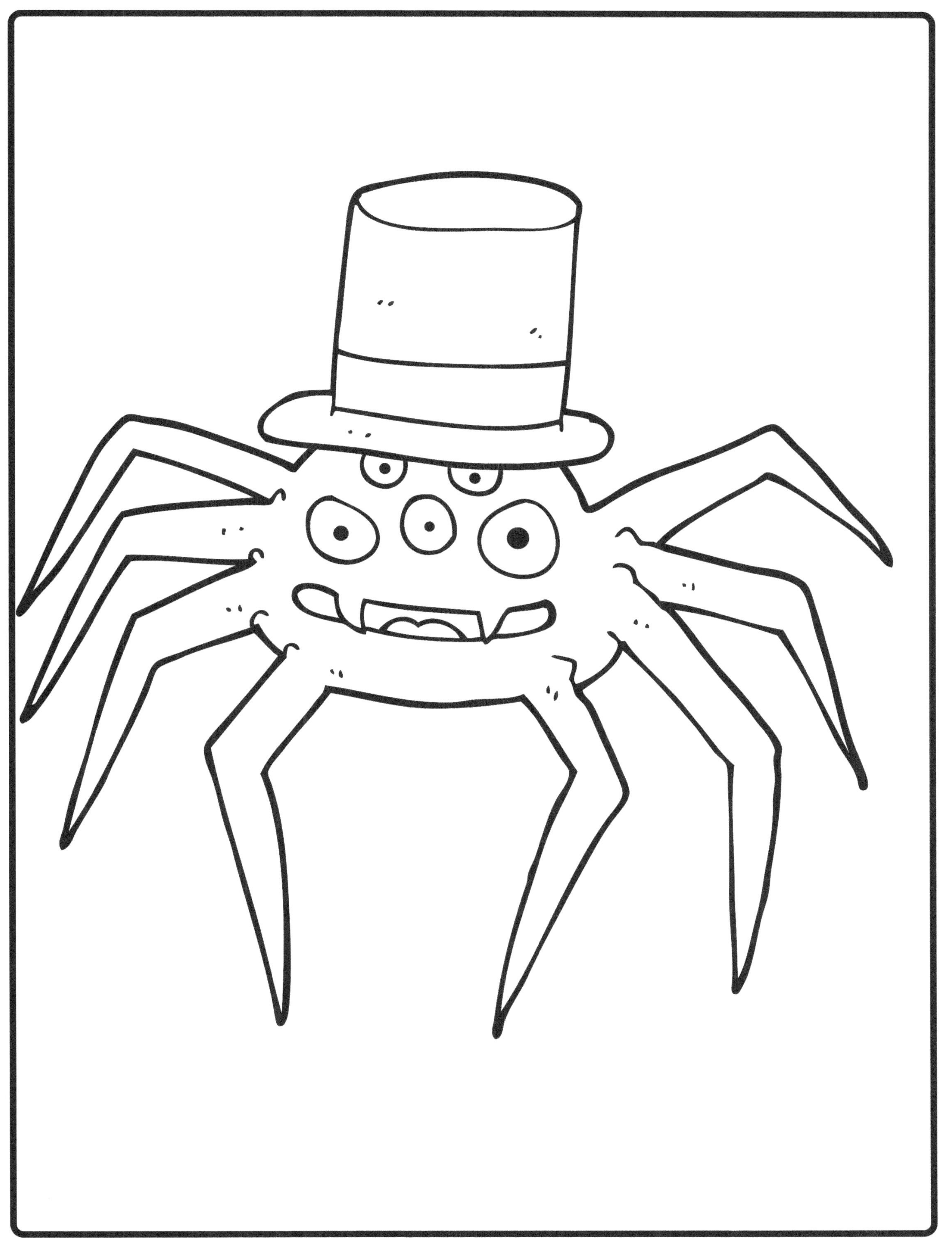

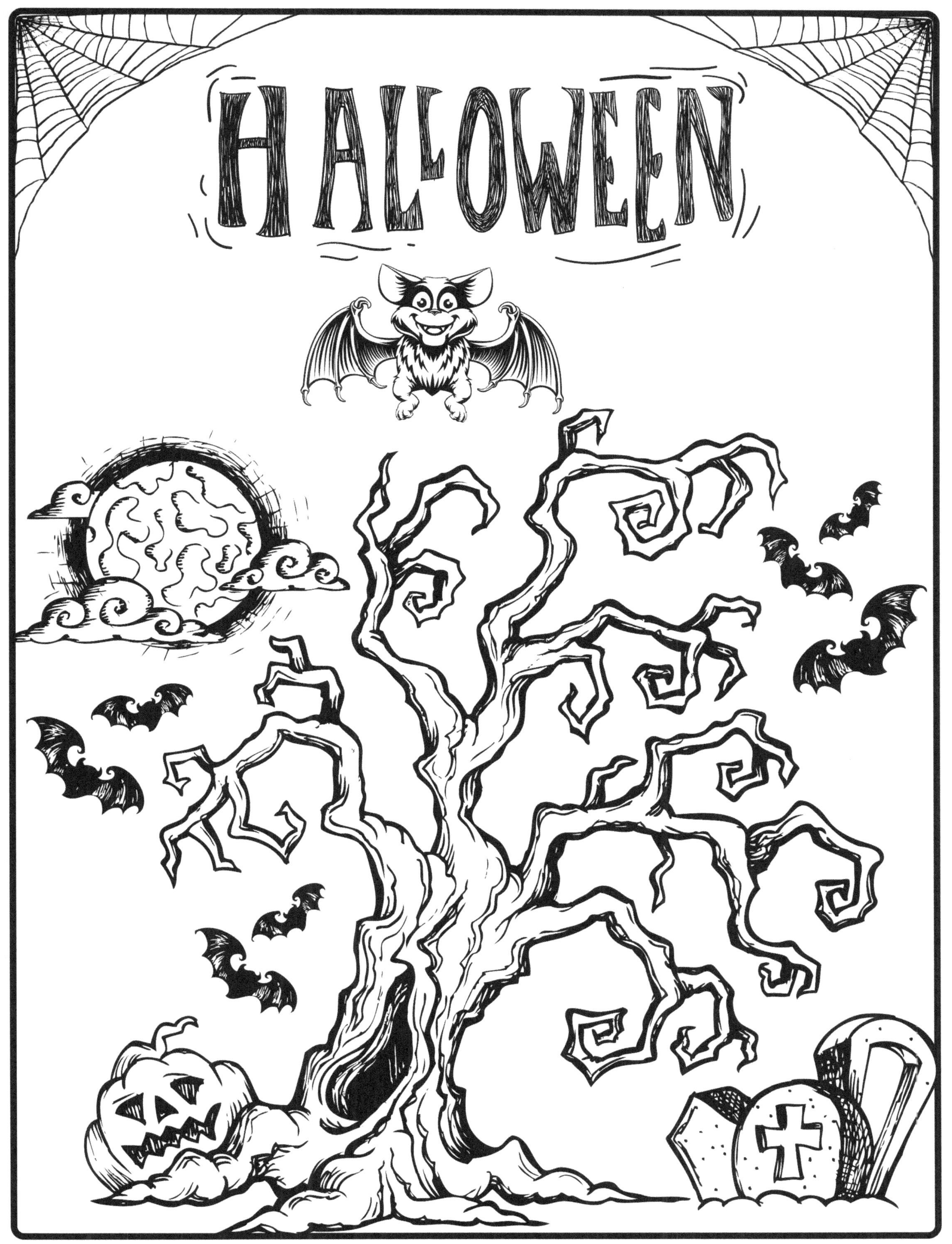
HALLOWEEN